MW00721368

JOURNALISM IN THE INFORMATION AGE

A Guide to Computers for Reporters and Editors

Brian S. Brooks

Missouri School of Journalism

Allyn and Bacon

Boston • London • Toronto • Sydney • Tokyo • Singapore

Vice President, Humanities: Joseph Opiela
Editorial Assistant: Kate Tolini
Marketing Manager: Karon Bowers
Editorial-Production Administrator: Donna Simons
Editorial-Production Service: Shepherd, Inc.
Composition and Prepress Buyer: Linda Cox
Manufacturing Buyer: Suzanne Lareau
Cover Administrator: Suzanne Harbison

Copyright © 1997 by Allyn & Bacon
A Viacom Company
160 Gould Street
Needham Heights, MA 02194

Internet: www.abacon.com
America Online: keyword: College Online

All rights reserved. No part of the material protected by this copyright notice may be reproduced or utilized in any form or by any means, electronic or mechanical, including photocopying, recording, or by any information storage and retrieval system, without written permission from the copyright owner.

Library of Congress Cataloging-in-Publication Data

Brooks, Brian S.
  Journalism in the information age : a guide to computers for
reporters and editors / Brian S. Brooks.
     p.   cm.
  Includes bibliographical references and index.
  ISBN 0–205–26411–5
  1. Journalism—Data processing. 2. Information networks.
3. Reporters and reporting.   I. Title.
PN4784'E5B76   1996
070.4'0285—dc20   96–26357
                                                          CIP

Printed in the United States of America

10 9 8 7 6 5 4 3 2 1   00 99 98 97 96

CONTENTS

PREFACE

I first became intrigued by the potential of computerized databases as a tool for working journalists in 1985. At the time I was managing editor of the *Columbia Missourian,* a small, Midwest, general-circulation daily that serves as a teaching laboratory for the world-famous Missouri School of Journalism.

In the early 1980s, the *Missourian*'s editors and librarians had been eager to subscribe to commercial database services such as Dialog, Vu/Text and Dow Jones News Retrieval, but the cost had been prohibitive. Now, however, fate had cast us a kind hand; an alumnus of the school had left a sizable bequest earmarked for improving the newspaper's library. We jumped at the chance to use the endowment income to subscribe to Dow Jones News Retrieval, our first online service, and eventually to others.

On the very day we received our Dow Jones password, the *Missourian*'s most computer-literate faculty editor, Phill Brooks, was working on a story about the pending award of a contract to set up Missouri's state lottery. Brooks, the state capital bureau chief, decided to see if Dow Jones contained any useful information on the companies bidding for the contract. There was an instant bonanza; one of the contenders had been investigated for ties to organized crime in several states. After making a few calls to confirm and flesh out the story, the story was in hand.

It made for a juicy headline atop Page One the next morning. What made it even better was that no other paper in the state, including the big-city papers in St. Louis and Kansas City, had the story. At a small paper, one lives for those moments. In this case, the "scoop" of statewide significance was directly attributable to Dow Jones.

That experience made me a big believer in the power that database services give to reporters and editors. Such services put a vast array of background information at their fingertips. Further, database services are more convenient and easier to use than traditional libraries. There often is no time for a visit to the local library when a reporter or editor is researching a story and deadlines loom, but with online database services only a phone call away, the absence of a database check is becoming inexcusable.

Today, I believe strongly that a reporter or editor who does not make regular use of such services is guilty of nothing less than professional malpractice. Newspapers or broadcast stations that tolerate ignorance of online services by reporters and editors could easily lose a lawsuit. What if a simple check of a commercial database service could have prevented the appearance of a libelous story? Would the failure to check constitute negligence? In my view, if it does not already, it soon will.

Further, I believe that failure to train aspiring reporters and editors in the use of databases and other computer technologies constitutes an intolerable gap in their educations. No journalism school or department worth attending could possibly ignore such training in a modern curriculum.

In saying that, however, I recognize that not every newspaper, broadcast station or school is fortunate enough to have an endowment to pay for online search costs. Some must control those costs by allowing only trained librarians to access online services, which often charge by the length of time one is connected.

While it would be great if all students, reporters and editors had access to the many online services directly from their computer workstations, that may be cost-prohibitive. However, it is not a problem if deans, department chairs, publishers and broadcast station managers make sure of the following:

- Commercial, online database services are available to someone in the newsroom or library who can help reporters with their searches. Often, the librarian assumes this role.
- Students, reporters and editors are sufficiently trained to know what online services might do for them. It does no good to have services available if the student, reporter or editor does not know when a search might help.

There is another reason for journalists to learn about computerized information retrieval services; increasingly, some of them are competitors to the existing media. In the months and years ahead, these *new media,* as they have come to be known, will continue to grow in influence. Because these new media are computer-based, easily accessible and updated 24 hours a day, consumers no longer have to wait for the next broadcast newscast or the delivery of the morning paper for news and other information. With a computer and modem, that consumer easily can tap into the vast databases of the Associated Press, United Press International, Reuters and others at any time of day or night and retrieve information on demand.

Further, on the electronic bulletin boards and chat areas of such services, consumers can talk with others who share their avid interest in topics as obscure as butterflies or as fascinating as genealogy. To the interested consumer, the information obtained from those forums is as much news as the material AP provides. Additionally, by going directly to such services, the consumer eliminates the journalist as a gatekeeper to information or, at the very least, reduces the journalist's role in that process. Whether that is good or bad is debatable, depending on one's perspective. Without question, though, the media of the future will allow consumers to make their own choices about what to see or read with little or no intervention by journalists.

In this book, we accept convention and refer to those services as the *new media*. However, various flavors of the new media are evolving, and their popularity to date is limited to users of personal computers. What they share is a common base of computers and digital communication through *cyberspace,* a catchy if somewhat vague way of referring to the wonderful world of computer networks and online databases.

In many ways, the arrival of computer-delivered information heralds the dawn of a new era for journalism and journalists. In writing this book, I intend, in some small way, to help students and journalists become acquainted with these emerging new electronic services. Only by understanding their power and potential can journalists adapt to the changing realities of the so-called Information Age.

No book can possibly reveal all one needs to know about the wide world of commercial databases, the Internet and the many other potential uses of computers in journalism. Without question, other books are more comprehensive. That is not the goal here; instead, I hope to produce a primer. My hope is to introduce the subject and in the process persuade those who read this book to venture into the vast world of online resources. Only by exploring and experimenting can one begin to recognize the potential of the resource. This book is intended not as a definitive history of new media but as a working companion to news writing and editing books, most of which treat the subject only casually.

My hope is that this book will introduce both students and working journalists to the exciting resource of commercial databases. Further, I hope it will serve as an introduction to the wonderful world of the Internet, which can be of huge benefit to journalists as an information resource. I also hope to acquaint them with the role of computer-based information services as an entirely new medium. Finally, I hope it will introduce both students and journalists to the many other ways in which computers can help them do a better job.

In addition, my appreciation is extended to colleagues from colleges and universities who reviewed the manuscript at its various stages: Douglass J. Carr, St. Bonaventure University; Thomas Donohue, Virginia Commonwealth University; John Newhagen, University of Maryland; and Donald Zimmerman, Colorado State University.

B.S.B.

1

THE CASE FOR USING COMPUTERS IN JOURNALISM

The occasion was a national meeting of newspaper editors. The year was 1993. A well-known editor of a major East Coast newspaper was speaking, and he was arguing forcefully that newspapers were losing circulation because they were losing touch with their readers. Then he entered waters that, for him at least, were uncharted.

> *Another big problem is that newspapers have become fascinated with computers. So have journalism schools. I guarantee you that I can run my newsroom without a single computer, and I'll put out a better newspaper than you can. And there's not a journalism school in this country that needs to invest in computers. What young reporters need to learn is how to gather information and write, and you don't need a computer to do either one.*

The assertion was so totally absurd that several in the audience were prompted to get up and leave the room. Muttered one upon exiting: "With guys like that running things, you wonder if newspapers *have* a future."

That computer-phobic editor is still quite active in the business, so we'll spare him the embarrassment of connecting his name with those comments. His remarks were so ludicrous they evoked memories of the story about an aging carpenter who insisted on cutting wood with a hand saw.

> *"I never had any use for a power saw," he said. "I can build a house just as well with a hand saw."*
>
> *"Sure," replied his young apprentice. "But with a power saw I can build one in one-tenth the time."*

Figure 1.1   Computers dominate today's newspaper and television newsrooms.

In the case of the newspaper editor, by spouting off without thinking he was ignoring at least two critical realities:

- Newsroom computers capture the keystrokes of reporters and editors, eliminating the need for rekeyboarding that took place in the "good old days" when reporters wrote on manual typewriters (see Figure 1.1). Without computers, newspapers would have to hire people to fill all those positions eliminated in the computer revolution. One hates to think how many U.S. newspapers that might make unprofitable.
- Computers make it possible for reporters to cover stories that were simply impossible to write in simpler times. It would take several reporters several lifetimes to do the data analyses done on computers that led to many of the recent Pulitzer Prizes in investigative reporting. Many similar computer analyses did not win Pulitzers. An example from the *St. Louis Post-Dispatch:**

*Reprinted with permission of the *St. Louis Post-Dispatch,* copyright 1990.

A man named Admiral Wherry, an Army veteran who owned a bar-becue pit and tire repair shop in East St. Louis, died more than two years ago.

But that didn't stop him from voting in the Illinois Democratic primary on March 20.

Wherry was one of at least five dead people in East St. Louis whose names were on the list of voters casting ballots in that Democratic primary, the Post-Dispatch *found. Those five are among at least 27 dead people who have voted posthumously in 17 of the past 26 elections there since 1981.*

Altogether, the Post-Dispatch *found 270 dead people who are registered in East St. Louis to vote in the election Nov. 6 that will decide the next governor of Illinois. Most of them died in Missouri.*

Besides these dead people, the Post-Dispatch *sampled five of the city's 50 precincts and found 113 people registered to vote from vacant lots or abandoned buildings. Sixteen of them voted in the March primary.*

. . . The city appears to have at least 2,700 ineligible voters, based on an estimate of voting age population. And from all indications, there are thousands more.[1]

Later in the story, the *Post-Dispatch* explained how it conducted its investigation:

The Post-Dispatch *used a computer to match property records and death certificates with a list of voters that the city provided to the state after the primary in March. Then, reporters verified computer records by examining paper records and vacant lots.*

The story is the type sure to attract public attention and cause great embarrassment to public officials. After all, the election process is something that Americans are supposed to hold sacred. Such a story also represents the type of watchdog reporting in which newspapers take pride; newspapers, editors often say, exist to keep public officials honest.

Imagine how difficult it would have been, however, to conduct that investigation without computers. The task of going through a list of more than 30,000 voters in East St. Louis would have been a chore in itself, not to mention matching those names with the property tax rolls and death records in two states. Indeed, until personal computers invaded the industry in the 1980s, such a story would have been unthinkable.

One wonders how our computer-phobic editor would have handled *that* story. Yes, it's true that one can learn to gather news and write without computers. In today's newsroom environment, however, don't expect to remain competitive with other reporters very long without regularly using computers. It is simply impossible for today's reporter to be as effective as possible while remaining ignorant about the world of information available at the touch of a computer keyboard.

Nor is it wise, as some still do, to think of the computer as exclusive property of the investigative journalist. Indeed, in today's best newsrooms computer searches of internal and external databases are an essential part of reporting *every* story. Some examples:

- *The morgue.* Anyone who has ever taken a journalism class remembers being told by a teacher: "When you are assigned to a story, begin in the morgue (the newspaper or broadcast station library). See what's already been written about the topic." That was good advice in the days when journalism libraries contained thousands of frayed, yellow clippings, and it remains good advice today, when libraries are computerized. Without using computers, how does one access a computerized library? Also, reporters are not the only ones who use the morgue; editors use it to check facts in a story, much as more traditional reference books are used.
- *Commercial databases.* Several companies operate databases that contain millions of newspaper, magazine and broadcast stories done by media from coast to coast. These databases give reporters and editors an opportunity to see what has been written or broadcast about a topic elsewhere. Consulting those sources broadens the scope of the background research conducted within the files of the newspaper's own library. Such checks help reporters and editors avoid missing key aspects of a story.
- *Government databases.* As the *Post-Dispatch* story shows, there's a world of information available about the people's business on governmental databases. It is almost inconceivable that a reporter can do a good job without regularly tapping these sources, from census data to agricultural crop data to Federal Aviation Agency airplane maintenance records. Those sources are not always used for investigative reporting. When an airplane crashes in your area, wouldn't it be useful to have instant access to the maintenance record of that aircraft? Of course it would, and it is possible with a knowledge of computers.
- *The Internet.* Much has been written about the role of the Internet as a precursor to the information superhighway envisioned by Vice President Al Gore and others. Today's journalist need not wait for that superhighway to be built. With the Internet, it's already here. Most federal government databases, and a growing number of state

and local ones, can be accessed via the Internet; so, too, can thousands of university computers in virtually every country around the world. Each of them is a veritable gold mine of information for the journalist who has learned to navigate the Internet (see Figure 1.2).

- *CD-ROMs.* The CD-ROM also has become a resource of note for journalists. In recent years, almost every conceivable type of information has been placed on these small computer-accessible disks. Collectively, they represent a wealth of information of great use to journalists. Moreover, CD-ROMs are becoming a publishing medium, ideal for combining text, full-motion video and sound. From multimedia encyclopedias to multimedia accounts of a presidential election, CD-ROMs have blossomed into a multibillion-dollar industry.

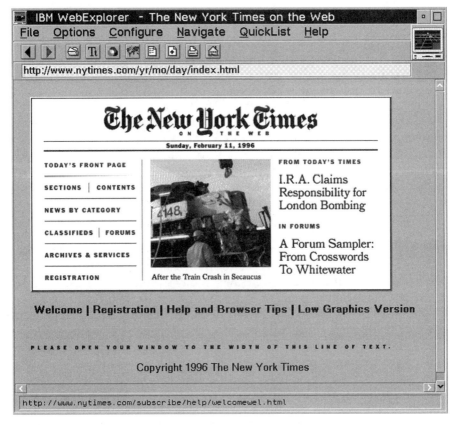

Figure 1.2 Even *The New York Times* has a site on the Internet today. The *Times'* site began getting 800,000 to 1 million hits a day immediately after launch.

Copyright © 1996 by The New York Times Co. Reprinted by permission.

Good journalism professors and good editors teach that factual information, including statistics, makes stories more credible. Databases of the types listed previously give the reporter access to thousands of sources of data that can be used to add credibility to a story. But to think of such sources as the province of only investigative or government reporters is a big mistake. Agriculture, business and lifestyle reporters can also make good use of such sources. The way today's government agencies store everything on computers, even the obituary writer needs to know about government databases; mortality statistics can be found there, too.

Not everything, of course, can be found in computer databases, government or nongovernment. Today's best reporters often solve that problem by creating their own.

When Elliot Grossman of the *Allentown* (Pa.) *Morning Call* wanted to document the fixing of parking tickets for Allentown police officers, the local Parking Authority refused access to its computerized records. But the paper records were available, and with the help of a news clerk and reporting interns, Grossman entered all the data from parking tickets by hand. While time-consuming work, the database that resulted enabled Grossman to document what he suspected: In Allentown, any excuse was enough to get a police officer off the hook for a parking violation.[2]

Grossman and others have used simple, off-the-shelf database software programs to do such work. Others have turned to computer spreadsheets to help. A government reporter, for example, might use a spreadsheet to compare trends in funding state agencies. By entering several years of appropriations data into a spreadsheet, it might be possible to spot spending trends, upward or downward, that otherwise might escape detection. Business reporters can do the same with corporate data.

Today's best reporters and editors have learned that computers can help in almost any phase of the reporting and editing process. They see computers as essential tools of the journalist's trade. Just as today's carpenters must learn to use power saws, today's journalists must learn to use computers. Failure to do so is a prescription for failure. The carpenter who uses only a hand saw soon will be put out of business by a more efficient competitor using a power saw. The journalist who does not use a computer will soon will be eclipsed by one who uses a computer to make a story more complete.

ENDNOTES

1. Tim Novak and George Landau, "Dead or Alive: City's Ineligible Voters Number in the Thousands," *St. Louis Post-Dispatch*, 1990.
2. Elliot Grossman, "Looking for Illegal Parking," *IRE Journal* 17:4, July–August 1994.

2

ONLINE COMMUNICATION: HOW IT WORKS

For the novice computer user, the world of bits, baud rates, modems, communications networks and asynchronous transmission can be intimidating. Fortunately, it is becoming less important for the user to understand how things work because vendors are isolating the user from much of that. Because that isolation is still far from total, however, let us review some of the basics.

MODEMS AND COMMUNICATIONS SOFTWARE

A *modem* (short for modulator-demodulator) is a device that permits one computer to talk with another across standard telephone lines. Modems connect to the telephone line with standard RJ-11 telephone jacks, the type used in most modern homes. Some modems are internal, which means they go inside your computer, and some are external devices that sit alongside your computer. External modems tend to cost a bit more because they must have their own power supplies. However, they do not take up an expansion slot inside your computer, so if slots are precious, an external modem is a good choice.

External modems connect to the computer through a *serial port*. Serial ports use both 9-pin and 25-pin connectors, so it is important to know which kind your computer uses before purchasing the cable used to connect the modem to your computer. Once your modem is installed, you are ready to add communications software.

Some commercial online services, including America Online, CompuServe, Prodigy and Nexis/Lexis, provide users with proprietary software to connect to their services. Typically, software of that type simplifies the installation process because there is no need for the user to set communications parameters. Those parameters may be confusing, and they must be set exactly for things to work properly. Bulletin boards, mainframes and similar systems require the user to supply the communications software. The best-seller in the United States among generic communications software programs is ProComm Plus. Plenty of other commercial programs also exist for that purpose, including Crosstalk and Smartcom. In addition, computer bulletin boards are full of shareware communications programs, which allow prospective users to download the software, test it, and then cast it aside or pay a small fee for its use. All are capable of performing *terminal emulation,* which allows a personal computer to act like a mainframe terminal when connected to a large mainframe computer by modem.

When you are required to set communications parameters, you will be asked for the word length (seven or eight data bits), the parity (even, odd or none) and the number of stop bits (usually one or none). If you do not know the parameters of the service you are calling, try 8-N-1 (eight data bits, no parity, one stop bit). Those are the most common settings, and most bulletin boards use them. Once you have discovered the correct parameters, your software program should allow you to store them for future use. That will make it unnecessary to go through this routine each time you call.

Of course, you will also need to know the best access number to use when connecting to the service you want to use. Most of the major commercial services offer connections through local telephone numbers in cities of more than 50,000 people. In smaller cities, you may be charged long-distance rates to connect, and that can significantly increase your monthly costs. Some services offer toll-free 800 numbers, but typically a surcharge is levied for using them. Still, that may be cheaper than paying regular long-distance rates. If you plan to do a lot of online work, it is a good idea to make a careful analysis of phone charges to determine the least expensive ways to connect.

Once you have set up your modem, connected it to your computer, installed your software and set your communications parameters, you are ready to enter the world of online communication. If you are a novice user, you probably should start by connecting to one of the easy-to-use commercial services such as America Online or CompuServe (see Chapter 3). As your confidence grows, you can branch out to the commercial services, the more arcane bulletin boards or the Internet.

UNDERSTANDING MODEMS

Computers are digital devices, which means everything they process must be expressed in numerical form. Internally, a computer uses a binary number system to describe each character (letter, number or symbol) it is capable of understanding. Each of those characters is expressed as a special sequence of binary *bits*. For example:

A = 01000001
B = 01000010

Those eight-bit collections of numbers are known as *bytes* of data, so eight bits equal a byte. The convention used to define characters is known as *ASCII* (American Standard Code for Information Interchange). ASCII is the common transmission language used by most computers. Computers understand only two things—on and off, or, in this case, 0 and 1. Data are transmitted from one device to another bit by bit. Because the sending computer and the receiving computer both understand the language of bits and bytes, they can communicate.

The problem is that computers know and understand *digital* signals while common telephone lines use *analog* signals. Digital signals have only two states (on or off; 0 or 1), whereas analog signals vary greatly (see Figure 2.1). That is why modems are essential. The modem on the transmission side serves as a *modulator* to convert digital signals into

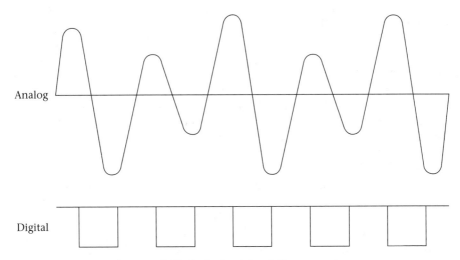

Figure 2.1   Analog and digital signals differ greatly.

analog. On the receiving end, the modem serves as a *demodulator,* converting analog signals into digital.

For this communication to occur, two modems must acknowledge each other's presence by establishing a *carrier signal.* If you have listened to the process of modems connecting through a modem's speaker (not all have them), you have heard what sounds like a rush of static, followed by silence. When the silence occurs, the modems have connected and the carrier signal is established. The silence is in fact a continuous audible tone. Your modem simply shuts off its speaker so you will not be distracted by it.

During the process of connecting, the two modems will determine that each is running at the same speed. Typically, both will connect at the highest *baud rate,* or speed, that the slowest of the two is capable of achieving. In recent years, the most common communication speed has increased from 300 baud to 1200 to 2400 to 9600 to 14,400 and now to 28,800 baud. Today's 28.8 modems, as they are known, are inexpensive, and buying one with a slower maximum speed makes little sense. For character-mode work, 9600-baud modems are quite adequate. But if you plan to connect to the Internet and use graphical interfaces such as Mosaic or Netscape, speed will be extremely important. In short, buy the fastest modem you can afford.

You will hear people speak of *asynchronous* and *synchronous* communications. In asynchronous communication, start and stop bits are used to define each character. In synchronous communication, a group of characters or block of data is sent as a continuous stream of bits. For most users, the distinction is irrelevant; almost all the communication journalists are likely to use is asynchronous.

Even higher-speed links are now available. Telephone companies in many major cities now offer *Integrated Services Digital Network* (ISDN) service. ISDN provides users with communications speeds more than 10 times faster than those offered by the fastest 28.8 modems. Wild differences in pricing and availability from area to area have hampered the spread of ISDN services. Some phone companies have discovered, though, that even home users are willing to pay $30 a month for a reliable, high-speed service. As a result, prices are dropping and availability is spreading.

The telephone companies also are rolling out ISDN because they are worried about pending competition from the cable television companies. New *cable modems* make it possible to deliver digital services over cable lines. The potential of such services is enormous because of the high capacity that cable television lines can provide. They are, after all, capable of delivering hundreds of television signals at a time. However, many cable systems were not designed for two-way communications, and the cable companies are being forced to make huge investments in their infrastructure to adapt to digital services. Look for a massive battle in the years ahead as the telephone and cable companies fight it out for the right to provide a digital connection to your home. The stakes are enormous. Both ISDN and cable-based services make it possible to deliver a powerful combination of text, graphics, audio and full-motion video that many see as the dominant news and information medium of the future.

NETWORK-BASED COMMUNICATIONS

Not all computer communication occurs through a modem attached to your computer. If you work at an office that has a *local area network,* or LAN, your computer may well contain all it needs to communicate with the outside world. Most likely, that communication will occur through your company's own multisite computer network, in the case of large corporations, or through the Internet.

Network communications require some sort of transmission protocol to permit computers to talk with external computers. In effect, such protocols eliminate the need for modems. The best-known of these is called *Transmission Control Protocol/Internet Protocol* (TCP/IP). If your corporate network has TCP/IP connections, with the appropriate software on your computer you can communicate through the Internet (see Chapter 5).

That is done through a shared high-speed link to the Internet. Many corporations and universities connect to the Internet this way at what the telephone companies refer to as T-1 speeds. That means the connection line is capable of handling about 1.5 megabits of data per second. That is much, much faster than modem speeds, so Internet links of this sort can be extremely efficient. Downloads of large computer programs take seconds, not minutes, through T-1 links. Even faster T-3 links are now available. Some newspapers, magazines and broadcast stations have slower connections to the Internet, perhaps through lines that carry 56 kilobits per second (often called *Switched 56* service). ISDN lines also are used for this purpose at small companies.

No discussion about modems and computer-based communication would be complete without reference to the issue of *bandwidth*. Standard telephone lines were intended for voice communication. *Voice-grade lines,* as they are called, can handle modem-to-modem communications quite well. However, twisted-pair copper lines used to connect telephones are limited in bandwidth, and therefore in the amount of traffic they can handle.

Fiber optics connections, or, more likely, cable television lines, eventually may provide greater bandwidth into the home. When that occurs, expect to see a boom in such services as movies on demand. Multimedia news programming will not be far behind. Before that happens, though, cable companies have lots of work to do to make their systems capable of supporting two-way traffic.

Those T-1, T-3 and ISDN lines referred to earlier are in effect conditioned circuits free of interference that can slow communication, a common phenomenon on voice-grade lines. Poor connections can severely restrict data throughput. In fact, even if your modem is capable of 28.8 transmission, if the phone lines are poor your modem will detect that and drop to a slower speed to ensure reliable communication. Because of that glitch, communication to remote areas or foreign countries with poor phone lines can be extremely tricky.

If all this sounds perplexing, do not let it deter you. You will find many friends who already have negotiated the minefields of online communication. Ask for help, and you are sure to find it.

3

EXPLORING THE PUBLIC
INFORMATION UTILITIES

For the journalist seeking to become literate in the exploration of commercial online databases, there is no better place to begin than the public information utilities, or PIUs. These are online services that cater to
the general public, not necessarily journalists. However, in them can be
found a wealth of information of great use to journalists and areas that
allow journalists to interact with their readers and viewers.

The public information utilities include America Online, Compu-
Serve, Delphi, WOW!, GEnie, The Microsoft Network (MSNBC) and
Prodigy. Most have various pricing plans that range from base service for
as little as $4.95 a month for limited usage to advanced charges that may
be substantially higher. It is not uncommon for novice users, suddenly
addicted to the services, to be surprised with bills of $150 or more for the
first month of usage. While basic rates are low, surcharges for faster
modem access or special services may drive up rates quickly.

One Prodigy user, addicted to that service's genealogy forum,
revealed that a recent bill for one month of service exceeded $150
because of his penchant for chatting online with others who shared his
interest. Asked how he could afford such extravagance, he replied, "I
can't. I've been taking the money out of savings, and if my wife finds out
she'll kill me." Online services are clearly addictive, so perhaps there is a
need for a PIUs Anonymous group—a cyberspace parallel to Alcoholics
Anonymous. Still, even with the explosive growth of the Internet, the
PIUs remain quite popular. Let us explore each of them in more detail,
highlighting their potential journalistic uses. They are listed in order
from most to least valuable, in the author's view, as both carriers for
major news services and as sources of information for journalists.

COMPUSERVE

For an exploratory trip through the PIUs, there is no better place for the journalist to begin than the Journalism Forum on CompuServe, the pioneer of the PIU services.

In that forum can be found a public online discussion of topics of interest to journalists, journalism students and educators. Discussion groups can be found in the message areas, and each message area is complemented by a library that contains textual information or programs of use to journalists. Like all areas in CompuServe, the forum can be accessed easily by entering a fast-path name at the appropriate prompt (Go JFORUM).

In Message Area 6, Radio and Television News, you can expect to find discussions about the coverage of major events, discussions about so-called "happy talk" news formats and almost anything else of interest to broadcast journalists. The related library section contains programs that allow columnar scripting for television scripts and other useful material.

Other message areas and libraries cover such topics as how to find jobs, "tricks of the trade," journalism ethics, future media and newsroom computers. Still others cover graphics and design, science and medical writing, and other topics.

In the Journalism Forum, journalists network with other journalists. As fascinating as that may be, other uses of CompuServe are even more exciting. Take, for example, forums that allow journalists and the public to communicate. Cable News Network has teamed with CompuServe to create forums that allow subscribers to interact with CNN anchors, access program listings (Go CNNFORUM) and ask questions during a daily news talk show (Go TALKBACK). *TalkBack Live,* as the show is called, allows viewers to ask questions by phone, fax or the TalkBack Live Forum on CompuServe. A studio audience also participates.

Print publications have not been left behind, as the presence of numerous magazines attests. Early adopters of the technology, perhaps predictably, were the computer magazines, including *MacWeek, PC World, PC Magazine* and *PC Computing.* Now, titles include mainstream publications such as *U.S. News & World Report* and Germany's *Der Spiegel.* Articles from the publications can be found there, but just as important are the exchanges that take place between journalists and subscribers on their forums. Notes CompuServe magazine:

> *Interactive publications . . . have become a means by which the cyberpublic can access editors and reporters who create their favorite reads. Open for discussion are not only recent articles but the implications of such news and how the stories came to be reported in the first place.*[1]

Further, reporters have begun using such forums to find quotable news sources. Reporters looking for veterans to interview on the 50th anniversary of D-Day merely posted their interest on CompuServe, and hundreds of responses came flowing in.

Newspapers have not been left behind, either. On CompuServe one can find the news archives of dozens of newspapers from the *Sacramento Bee* to the *St. Louis Post-Dispatch* and *Florida Today.* CompuServe's extracost premium service, called the Executive News Service (for information, Go EXECUTIVE), gives subscribers access to 23 wire services, including the Associated Press, United Press International, Reuters, AP France, Deutsche Press-Agentur, the Australian Associated Press, PR Newswire and the Dow Jones News Service. That is a treasure trove of current information.

One interesting feature of CompuServe's Executive News Service (Go ENS) is its clipping service (see Box). Subscribers merely define areas of interest, and the service scans all 23 news wires each day to find articles on those topics. The found articles then are stored in folders for the user to access at a convenient time.

CompuServe is easiest to navigate using the CompuServe Information Manager software available for DOS, Windows, OS/2 or the Macintosh operating systems (see Figure 3.1), or third-party software programs such as OzCIS, Golden CommPass and TAPCIS, which accomplish the same thing. However, the service also is available in ASCII text form or through terminal emulation for those without one of today's popular GUIs (graphical user interfaces).

Because CompuServe is the oldest of the PIUs, it is comprehensive in its content. Its forums are extremely active, and as a result CompuServe is a great place to find experts or people interested in almost every conceivable subject. On the other hand, its graphic appeal is not quite up to the standards of America Online, which has attracted more interactive newspapers. In comparison, CompuServe has the look and feel of an archival service. Indeed, much of its newspaper content usually appears a day or two after printed publication and therefore is unsuitable as a source of breaking news. On Prodigy and America Online, newspaper content is posted as quickly as it is published and sometimes even before. Still, with its extensive wire service offerings, magazines and other services, CompuServe is an essential part of the journalist's online portfolio.

A word of caution is in order: CompuServe's pricing structure makes heavy use of this service much more expensive than America Online or Prodigy.

For information contact CompuServe Inc., 5000 Arlington Centre Blvd., P.O. Box 20212, Columbus, OH 43220, tel. (800) 848–8199.

Creating Folders in CompuServe's Executive Information Service

Using CompuServe Information Manager for DOS, Windows or OS/2

1. Go ENS and select the *Stories* menu option from the top of the screen. Select *Create Folder*.
2. A *Create Folder* box will be displayed. In that box, select folder search criteria, newspapers from which you want to "clip," the number of days stories should be retained and the folder's expiration date (no longer than one year).
3. At any time, select the *Help* key or press F1 to receive helpful instructions.

Using CompuServe Information Manager for Macintosh

1. Go ENS and click on the *Maintain Folders* icon.
2. A box entitled *Personal Folders* will appear. Click on the *Add* button.
3. An *Add a New Folder* box will appear. Follow the instructions for the *Create Folder* box above.
4. At any time, click on the question mark icon at the top right corner of the box to receive help.

Using an ASCII or Terminal Emulation Program

1. Type Go ENS and select Option 4, *Create/Change/Delete a Personal Folder (E)* from the ENS main menu.
2. Choose Option 1, *Create a Personal Folder*.
3. Answer the subsequent questions, including the name you want to give the folder, its expiration date (no longer than one year), the number of days up to 14 that stories should be retained in the folder and the news wires you want included.
4. Enter up to seven keywords.

Adapted from CompuServe Magazine, November 1994. © CompuServe Incorporated.

AMERICA ONLINE

America Online ranks as the country's largest and fastest growing PIU. That is a direct result of its superior user interface (see Figure 3.2), which is attributable to the Windows- or Macintosh-based software the service provides free to new users, and its aggressive marketing. The software is the fastest and friendliest provided by any of the PIUs, and America Online has been aggressive in distributing it freely with magazines and through direct mail. The service also spends far more than its competitors on television advertising.

America Online was the early leader in attracting newspapers to its service. It did so as a means of filling what AOL executives considered a

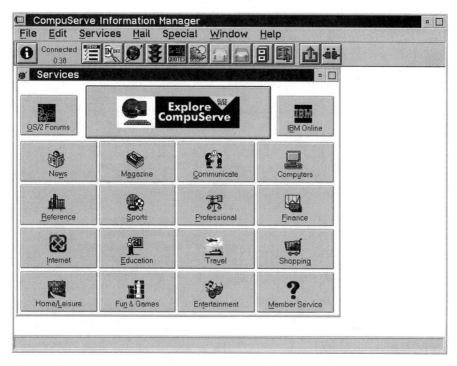

Figure 3.1 CompuServe Information Manager's opening screen makes it easy to navigate the service. CompuServe also can be accessed in character mode.

© CompuServe Incorporated.

major gap in online services—the absence of local news and information. Once America Online attracted the *Chicago Tribune* and *San Jose Mercury News* as early collaborators, services such as Prodigy and Delphi jumped onto the bandwagon and began signing up local partners, too. AOL has announced plans to provide massive amounts of local content in two hundred of the country's largest cities—with or without newspaper partners. Because local content is expected to be a key to winning and holding subscriptions, the move would appear to be a wise one for AOL.

Like CompuServe, America Online is a comprehensive service that contains forums on almost every conceivable topic. Without question, that makes it both a formidable competitor to CompuServe and an interesting source of information for journalists. However, America Online's most interesting feature for a journalist is its collection of top-rated newspapers, news magazines and broadcast services. The service contains the following items:

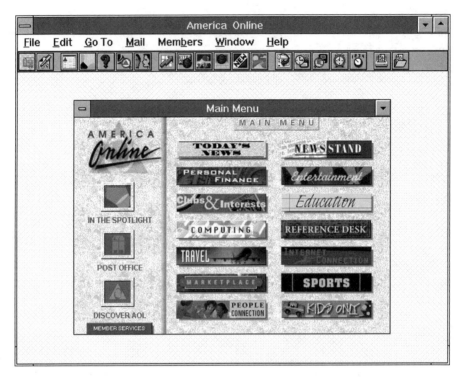

Figure 3.2 **America Online's main menu makes it easy to find your way through the service. News services and Internet access are prominently highlighted.**

Copyright 1996: America Online. Used by permission.

- @Times, an electronic version of *The New York Times.* This is one of the few places to get the best of the nation's most influential daily newspaper electronically on the day it is published, although the *Times* itself now operates a successful web site.
- ABC News on Demand, a complete information service from one of the nation's leading television networks.
- TIME magazine. While TIME also is experimenting with Internet distribution, this excellent newsmagazine service is accessible to more home users. The AOL version includes the full text of the current week's issue.[2]
- Capital Connection, a collection of interesting news sources from the nation's capital.

Those services are merely the start of what's available on America Online. Plenty of magazines can be found there, including such diverse titles as *Army Times, Boating* and *National Geographic Explorer.* AOL also has a thoughtful collection of material geared toward younger audiences, including the *Smithsonian Magazine.* Business-oriented users also get plenty of attention here with services that include *Investors Business Daily.*

Additionally, AOL is attempting to establish a significant presence in Europe with its European counterpart.

For information contact America Online, 8619 Westwood Center Drive, Vienna, VA 22182–2285, tel. (800) 827–6364.

PRODIGY

Prodigy originally was a venture of unlikely partners: CBS, Sears and IBM. From the outset, its aim was to provide a top-notch home-shopping service. CBS bailed out early, leaving Sears and IBM to make the service popular. Sears was to bring the retail marketing expertise, and IBM was to provide the technical know-how. In 1996, the two giants sold their interests in Prodigy after falling far behind CompuServe and Prodigy in number of subscribers. Prodigy has suffered greatly from slow software and lagging ability to provide high-speed access. In many smaller cities, Prodigy still offers only 9600-baud service while AOL and CompuServe offer 28.8 connections. So, while in many ways Prodigy's content makes it one of the more attractive PIUs, it has lost ground to the big two. Once almost even with AOL in memberships, it now trails so badly it may never catch up.

Prodigy has announced a strategy of migrating to the increasingly popular Internet. Only time will tell whether that strategy will save Prodigy or doom it to extinction.

Prodigy's strong content is often masked by the absence of a fast, responsive user interface and its uninviting screen designs (see Figure 3.3). Prodigy originally relied on built-in typefaces rather than those familiar to Macintosh and Windows users. When criticism from detractors caused that strategy to fail, Prodigy adopted a bland look that destroyed much of its character. The result is the absence of a truly attractive interface for the service.

Unique to Prodigy among the PIUs is the force-feeding of advertising. The bottom third of many Prodigy screens is an advertisement. Users can click on a button bar for more information about the product being sold. This pervasive approach to advertising has made Prodigy an industry leader in advertising revenue. Some users are repulsed by this heavy-handed approach, but the advertisements are popular with many

Figure 3.3 The Prodigy interface has been simplified to improve navigation of the service and to provide a more aesthetically pleasing look.

©1996 Prodigy Services Corporation. All rights reserved.

subscribers. As journalists know, consumers are often just as interested in advertisements as they are in news.

Despite its faults, those who dismiss Prodigy as an ugly, advertisement-laden mess would appear to be wearing blinders. If one ignores the blandness of Prodigy's design, the service's easy-to-use interface contains lots of shortcuts that make Prodigy easy for the novice to navigate.

Prodigy's news resources are both considerable and easy to use. And, while Prodigy once lagged in aligning with local news vendors, it has been catching up rapidly. The *Atlanta Journal and Constitution*'s Prodigy-based service, *Access Atlanta,* is by some accounts the most successful "online newspaper" of all. Prodigy also scored several coups with the addition of the online versions of the *Los Angeles Times* and *Newsweek* magazine, and an alliance with ESPN, the cable sports network, that makes Prodigy's coverage of breaking sports tough to match.

Prodigy's bulletin boards are among the industry's most heavily used, and their topics run the gamut. As a result, journalists will find plenty of potential news sources there.

For information contact Prodigy Services Co., 445 Hamilton Ave., White Plains, NY 10601, tel. (800) PRODIGY.

THE MICROSOFT NETWORK (MSNBC ONLINE)

Microsoft, the software giant, launched its online service in late 1995, pegged to the introduction of Windows 95. Since then, it has teamed with NBC to provide a news operation of considerable merit. In late 1995 the two companies announced that they would collaborate on two projects, the Microsoft Network and a new cable channel designed to challenge Ted Turner's Cable News Network. The joint venture is named MSNBC, and it is expected that the two companies will create a subsidiary to facilitate their collaboration. Expect massive cross-promotion between the cable channel and the online service as MSNBC seeks to carve out a significant share of both the online and cable news markets. Also look for significant promotion on NBC itself.

In creating MSN, Microsoft was sensitive to widespread attacks from the media about the idea of a software company entering the news business. To counter that criticism, the company hired a cadre of first-rate journalists and gave them plenty of freedom to create content. In fact, the criticism of Microsoft's venture is somewhat absurd given the competition. Is the idea of Microsoft owning a news company somehow more reprehensible than IBM and Sears owning Prodigy? Is it fundamentally different from the Walt Disney Co. owning ABC and newspapers? Even the big traditional news companies themselves are often so widely diversified and so bottom-line oriented that news simply is not understood in the boardroom. In any event, the joint venture with NBC quelled some of the criticism. In joining with an established news company, Microsoft bought a considerable amount of credibility.

At the moment, MSN still lacks the depth of content that the major PIUs offer, but with the company's vast resources combined with those of NBC, it could catch up quickly. Microsoft bundles access software with every copy of its Windows 95 program, and access software for other platforms is promised.

Microsoft claims to be committed to increasing revenue for its content providers. Typically, with services such as CompuServe and Prodigy, the content provider gets only 10 to 20 percent of the revenue while the

PIU gets the rest. Microsoft, if it really changes that, could be well-positioned to attract lots of information providers. Most agree that content is the key to selling online services. The better the content, the more likely consumers are to buy.

For information contact Microsoft Inc., 1 Microsoft Way, Redmond, WA 98052–6399, tel. (206) 882-8080.

DELPHI

Delphi's early development was limited by its absence of a Windows- or Macintosh-based user interface, a deficiency that finally has been corrected. On the other hand, it was the early leader in providing comprehensive access to the Internet, arguably the world's most important source of journalistic information (see Chapter 5).

Delphi is a leader in multiplayer online games, a subject of little interest to journalists unless that happens to be the topic of an article in progress. Delphi's strength for journalists lies in its top-notch Internet links and its comprehensive business coverage, which includes stock and commodity prices for more than 9,000 publicly traded issues (delayed by 15 minutes). Marketpulse, unique to Delphi, gives an immediate snapshot of the market with the current Dow Jones average, the most active stocks, advances and declines, and percentage of gains and losses. Still, other services are rapidly improving their business reporting, and Delphi is losing that edge.

As on the larger services, the journalist can find news sources on Delphi. However, don't expect the response level you might get on Prodigy or CompuServe. Delphi's subscriber base is substantially smaller. Nonetheless, it would be a mistake to dismiss Delphi as a player in the online market.

For information contact Delphi Internet Services Corp., 1030 Massachusetts Ave., Cambridge, MA 02138, tel. (800) 695–4005.

GENIE

GEnie until recently lacked a Windows-based, user-friendly interface, and it still lacks an interface for Macintosh users. While a Windows interface is now available, it is not as good as those for CompuServe or America Online. GEnie is rushing to provide full Internet access.

GEnie subscribers can access NBC Online, a roundtable that provides entertainment, sports and other information on the television network.

Users can provide the network with feedback on programs. Beyond that, there is little on GEnie of unique interest to journalists.

GEnie carved its niche in the market by becoming an electronic mail service for business users. It still has not found a compelling way to broaden its appeal, and it has only about 100,000 subscribers. That makes it a tiny, insignificant player in the online market, a factor that led General Electric to sell the service in early 1996 to Yovelle Renaissance Corp. of Queens, N.Y. Unless and until the new owners pump some life into the service, there is no good reason for a journalist to select it over one of the more popular ones.

For information contact General Electric Information Services, 401 N. Washington St., Rockville, MD 20849–6403, tel. (800) 638–9636.

THE FUTURE OF PIUs

The services listed previously, while the most common, certainly are not the only ones. A new one called The Transom (tel. [800] 475–9689) claims to be a hip alternative to the mainstream providers. Still, do not expect to see many more startups of proprietary online services. That is because the future of online services lies on the Internet. The PIUs doing the best today are those such as America Online that offer excellent access to the Internet's many sites.

Because of the Internet's growing importance, the future of the pub lic information utilities is a topic of great debate. Some fledgling PIU services, such as AT&T's Interchange, already have abandoned the PIU model in favor of a complete move to the Internet. Prodigy has indicated it may do the same. America Online and CompuServe have created simplified Internet-access services, called Global Network Navigator and WOW!, respectively, to provide simplified user access to the Internet using their proprietary networks as the access points. Setting up an account with a direct Internet access provider is invariably much more difficult.

BULLETIN BOARDS

All the services mentioned earlier are commercial, so it is only natural that their income allows them to provide an array of services unmatched by any free service. However, any discussion of online forums would be incomplete without a discussion of the thousands of computer bulletin boards constructed and maintained by passionate devotees of almost any topic imaginable.

Want information on adopting pets? Numerous bulletin boards address the topic. Interested in exploring cults for a news story? There are bulletin boards that specialize in the topic. Want information on federal agencies? Many maintain bulletin boards. As a result, journalists should not dismiss the bulletin board services as insignificant. The problem comes in trying to find a board with content of interest to you. A good place to start is with a subscription to *Online Access* magazine (5615 W. Cermak Road, Cicero, IL 60650–2290, tel. (800) 36-MODEM, 10 issues for $29.70). *Online Access* regularly provides updates on interesting BBS sites.

Your local computer store operator also can give you information on BBSs located in your area. That is a good way to get the feel of how a BBS operates without spending a lot of money on long-distance charges, which is a real danger with these services.

Some of the BBS services have grown to the point that they are commercial and advertise in magazines. One such service is Exec-PC (2105 S. 170th St., New Berlin, WI 53151, tel. [414] 789–4200 [voice]). It offers fairly comprehensive Internet access.

LOCAL COMMERCIAL SYSTEMS

One interesting development in online communication merits mention. Some information providers, including many newspapers, are selling Internet access and using their own content as a first point of presence there. Such services are gaining popularity and have one advantage that the PIUs cannot match—the ready availability of massive amounts of local news and information. Such services can be delivered less expensively than what one pays for a PIU, and as a result they pose a significant competitive threat. We will discuss those services in more detail in Chapter 5.

ENDNOTES

1. "It's News to Me," *CompuServe Magazine,* November 1994, p. 12.
2. *America Online Member Guide,* 1994, p. 14.

4

EXPLORING THE COMMERCIAL DATABASE SERVICES

Unlike the public information utilities, commercial database services are repositories of information marketed primarily to companies, not individuals. Typically, their graphical user interfaces are less appealing, if they even have such things, and they do not cater to the casual computer user. However, for archival information from most of the nation's big daily newspapers and magazines, these services cannot be matched.

The United States' primary commercial database services of interest to journalists are Dialog, Nexis/Lexis, Vu/Text, DataTimes, Dow Jones Information Retrieval and PressLink. Each has a different collection of repositories for user access, and they represent a veritable gold mine for the journalist doing background research for a story. Do not bother to look for bulletin boards or forums where people chat about dieting, though; these services are strictly business.

For a publication or broadcast station of any size at all, a subscription to one or more of these services is not a nicety but a necessity. It is inconceivable that a serious reporter would want to work at a newspaper, magazine or television station that didn't subscribe to Nexis/Lexis, VuText or DataTimes. In today's world, a reporter simply cannot do a good job without a commercial database service. The local library is a poor second choice; in comparison, it is difficult to use and not very convenient. As any newspaper or broadcast journalist knows, there seldom is time to run to the library to check a fact when you are working against deadline.

The problem is that the commercial services are expensive to use. As a result, small newspapers, magazines and broadcast stations cannot afford them, and their news stories suffer as a result. Most commercial services charge by the minute for connect time, and some even levy a surcharge based on the number of records retrieved from the database. Still others charge extra if you want to print a document. All of that adds up to a costly proposition for heavy users.

Many newspapers, magazines and broadcast stations try to control those costs by limiting access to certain individuals in the newsroom, which is often the librarian. Under this system, the reporter outlines to the librarian what he or she is trying to find. They talk a bit and settle on a search strategy, but the librarian actually does the search. The theory is that a trained librarian can do the search more quickly and efficiently than a relatively untrained reporter. That is probably true, and the process is unquestionably a good way to contain costs. However, such a system presents problems, too.

Much of what a reporter does involves following leads, and as any experienced reporter knows, a lot of those leads are not leads at all. Instead, they are dead ends. If the search system discourages these fishing expeditions, will big stories be missed? Yes, argue many reporters, some of whom have been able to convince management to spend the necessary money to provide commercial database access to all. Clearly, only large, profitable publications and broadcast stations are able to play in that league.

When newspapers, magazines and broadcast stations began using these services in earnest during the 1980s, investigative reporters led the way. They were intrigued with the power of being able to log on to Nexis/Lexis or Dialog and search hundreds of newspapers, instantaneously, for anything written about an individual. Let us say, for example, that a smooth operator blows into your city and announces his intention to build a track for thoroughbred racing. In the past, a check of his background might take months. Today, a simple check of the commercial databases might reveal—in a matter of minutes—a gambling-related conviction 12 years earlier in a city more than a thousand miles away. No time-consuming, drawn-out investigation would be necessary, and what might have required a months-long investigation instead would make the next edition or newscast. Viewed in that light, the use of commercial databases *saves* money that a lengthy investigation would have required.

So, while the use of commercial databases once was the province of the investigative reporter, today every reporter must use them. It is difficult to imagine any reporter on any beat who could not benefit by learning in a matter of moments what others have written about a subject.

If all this sounds terrific, it is. The use of commercial services has changed the way U.S. reporters work, but there also are some pitfalls. Be aware that there are limits on how much material you can use from other sources before the copyright law requires you to obtain written permission. The *fair-use rule* in U.S. copyright law permits you to quote a minor portion of a given work without permission. Knowing what constitutes fair use can be tricky, however. We will discuss that and other legal issues in more detail in Chapter 8.

While there may be legal problems, other problems may be just as troublesome. For example, when you take information from another source, it is secondhand information. Even if it comes from a respected publication such as *The New York Times,* there always is the chance that the *Times'* reporter made a mistake. Because of that danger, good reporters try to verify information with more than one source. Says one reporter who uses commercial databases frequently:

> *My worst nightmare is learning that something was written incorrectly and then repeated in newspapers and magazines nationwide. The way reporters use commercial databases these days, it's possible for an error to be picked up and multiplied many times over.*

That is a danger, to be sure. However, the benefits reporters gain from using the commercial services far outweigh the negatives. The use of such services is a rich resource that, when combined with good reporting skills, can make a good reporter a great one.

A TYPICAL SEARCH

Let us do a search of Nexis/Lexis to illustrate how useful these services can be to a journalist. In our example, you are a reporter assigned to write a story on the upcoming local appearance of actress Kate Capshaw in your community. You want some background information on her so you can ask some reasonably intelligent questions during the interview. A quick check of Nexis/Lexis reveals that a company named Gale Research Inc. provides biographical sketches of celebrities. Your search of that database produces this:*

```
                    LEVEL 1 - 1 OF 3 BIOS
              Copyright 1994 Gale Research, Inc.
                     All Rights Reserved
            Contemporary Theatre, Film and Television

                   August, 1994; Volume 12

LENGTH: 307 words

NAME:  Kate Capshaw

  PERSONAL:
    Original name, Kathleen Sue Nail; born in 1953, in Fort Worth, TX; married
John Capshaw (divorced); married Steven Spielberg (a director, producer, and
```

*Copyright © Gale Research. All rights reserved.

screenwriter), October 12, 1991; children: (first marriage) Jessica, (second marriage) Sasha.

ADDRESSES: Agent—International Creative Management, 8942 Wilshire Blvd., Beverly Hills, CA 90211.

EDUCATION: Attended University of Missouri.

CAREER:
Actress. Has worked as a schoolteacher.

MEMBERSHIPS:
Screen Actors Guild, American Federation of Television and Radio Artists.

CREDITS: FILM APPEARANCES (Debut) Katherine, A Little Sex, Universal, 1982. Willie Scott, Indiana Jones and the Temple of Doom, Paramount, 1984. Laura, Best Defense, Paramount, 1984. Dr. Jane DeVries, Dreamscape, Twentieth Century-Fox, 1984. Emily Reubens, Windy City, Warner Bros., 1984. Sydney Betterman, Power, Twentieth Century-Fox, 1986. Andie, Spacecamp, Twentieth Century-Fox, 1986. Brunetta, Ti Presento un'Amica, Medusa, 1988. Joyce Kingsley, Black Rain, Paramount, 1989. Mrs. Ellen McGraw, Love at Large, Orion, 1990. Jolie Meadows, My Heroes Have Always Been Cowboys, Samuel Goldwyn, 1991. TELEVISION APPEARANCES; MOVIES Elaine Rogers, Missing Children: A Mother's Story, CBS, 1982. Susanna McKaskel, The Quick and the Dead, HBO, 1987. Anne Goodwin, Her Secret Life (also known as One for the Dancer and Code Name: Dancer), ABC, 1987. TELEVISION APPEARANCES; EPISODIC "George Lucas: Heroes, Myths, and Magic," American Masters, PBS, 1993. OTHER TELEVISION APPEARANCES Joanna Gates, Internal Affairs (mini-series), CBS, 1988. Time Warner Presents the Earth Day Special, ABC, 1990. Shattered Lullabies (special; also known as Your Family Matters), Lifetime, 1992. Margo Cody, Black Tie Affair (series; also known as Smoldering Lust and The Girl in 1216), NBC, 1993.

Appeared in the series The Edge of Night, ABC.

LANGUAGE: ENGLISH

LOAD-DATE-MDC: July 27, 1994

Already you have discovered a mother lode of information about Kate Capshaw. You know that she was born in Fort Worth, attended the University of Missouri and worked as a schoolteacher. You also know that she has been married twice—currently to acclaimed movie director Steven Spielberg—and has one child by each husband. You also have a complete list of her acting credits and the name of her agent. With that alone, you are better-prepared for your interview. Let us see what else we can find.

A search of the major newspapers and magazines database within Nexis/Lexis reveals a list of 424 stories about Capshaw. You decide to look at some recent citations for something that might help.*

LEVEL 1 - 424 STORIES
1.   Chicago Tribune, December 27, 1994 Tuesday, NORTH SPORTS FINAL EDITION, NEWS; Pg. 16; ZONE: N; Arts Plus. East Coast '94. A look back., 1071 words, PARTY SMARTIES; IN CASE YOU MISSED 1994'S BIGGEST BASHES (JOIN THE CLUB), HERE'S WHAT YOU DIDN'T MISS, By Lisa Anderson and Michael Kilian, Tribune Staff Writers.

*Reprinted with the permission of LEXIS-NEXIS, a division of Reed Elsevier Inc. LEXIS and NEXIS are registered trademarks of Reed Elsevier Properties, Inc.

2.   The Toronto Star, December 13, 1994, Tuesday, FINAL EDITION, ENTERTAINMENT; Pg. B6, 823 words, Python to stay dead, says Cleese

3.   The New York Times, December 4, 1994, Sunday, Late Edition— Final, Section 6; Page 69; Column 1; Magazine Desk , 3179 words, IT'S . . . !; LIAM NEESON, By Dinitia Smith; Dinitia Smith is a novelist and journalist in New York.

4.   Newsday, November 27, 1994, Sunday, CITY EDITION, NEWS; INSIDE NEW YORK; Pg. 17, 6 words, The Week's Worth, By Michael Shain and Anthony Scaduto, COLUMN; GOSSIP; CELEBRITY

5.   Sunday Times, November 20, 1994, Sunday, Features, 905 words, Jumping to offer her support, Christa D'Souza

6.   Los Angeles Times, November 11, 1994, Friday, Home Edition, Calendar; Part F; Page 1; Column 5; Entertainment Desk, 1320 words, FILMMAKERS DOUBT GOP VICTORY WILL AFFECT WORK; MOVIES: MOST INDUSTRY INSIDERS SAY SUBJECT MATTER IS IMMUNE TO POLITICAL LANDSCAPE. STILL, MUCH OF HOLLYWOOD IS CASTING A WARY EYE TOWARD THE RISE IN CONSERVATIVES' POWER., By ELAINE DUTKA and ROBERT W. WELKOS, TIMES STAFF WRITERS

7.   Los Angeles Times, October 31, 1994, Monday, Home Edition, Life & Style; Part E; Page 5; Column 1; View Desk, 763 words, RSVP; ROYALTY, CELEBRITIES AT 'OSCARS OF CHARITY BALLS', By BILL HIGGINS, SPECIAL TO THE TIMES

8.   Los Angeles Times, October 25, 1994, Tuesday, Home Edition, Business; Part D; Page 1; Column 2; Financial Desk, 1150 words, THE BIZ / ALAN CITRON AND CLAUDIA ELLER: 'DREAM TEAM'S' 1ST PROJECT: MASTERING SPIN CONTROL, By ALAN CITRON and CLAUDIA ELLER

9.   The Washington Post, October 20, 1994, Thursday, Final Edition, STYLE; PAGE D3; THE RELIABLE SOURCE, 1069 words, THE RELIABLE SOURCE, Lois Romano, With Mary Alma Welch

10.   Forbes, October 17, 1994, THE FORBES FOUR HUNDRED; Over $ 600,000,000; Pg. 201, 127 words, Steven Allen Spielberg

11.   Los Angeles Times, October 17, 1994, Monday, Home Edition, Life & Style; Part E; Page 5; Column 3; View Desk, 419 words, INTO THE NIGHT: RSVP; A SOUND STAGE DRESSED FOR A BIG SUCCESS, By BILL HIGGINS, SPECIAL TO THE TIMES

12.   The New York Times, October 16, 1994, Sunday, Late Edition - Final Correction Appended, Section 1; Page 1; Column 2; National Desk, 2282 words, A Hollywood Recipe: Vision, Wealth, Ego, By BERNARD WEINRAUB with GERALDINE FABRIKANT, Special to The New York Times, HOLLYWOOD, Oct. 15

13.   USA TODAY, October 14, 1994, Friday, FINAL EDITION, LIFE; Jeannie Williams; Pg. 2D, 526 words, JFK Jr. makes the next move on magazine, Jeannie Williams

14.   Los Angeles Times, October 13, 1994, Thursday, Home Edition, Part A; Page 1; Column 4; Metro Desk, 2114 words, 'DREAM TEAM' TRIO OUTLINE PLANS FOR STUDIO, By ALAN CITRON and CLAUDIA ELLER, TIMES STAFF WRITERS

15.   USA WEEKEND, October 9, 1994, Sunday, Pg. 4, 1912 words, Warren & Annette's family values/Beatty & Bening, Jonathan Alter

16.   Los Angeles Times, October 6, 1994, Thursday, Home Edition, San Gabriel Valley; Part J; Page 10, 1701 words, SAN GABRIEL VALLEY/COVER STORY; REAL CLIFFHANGERS; TRAGEDY CAN BE JUST A STEP AWAY FOR THOSE WHO ENTER THE ANGELES NATIONAL FOREST UNPREPARED FOR ITS DEADLY VARIETY OF NATURAL HAZARDS., By KEVIN UHRICH, SPECIAL TO THE TIMES

17.   Los Angeles Times, October 3, 1994, Monday, Home Edition, Life & Style; Part E; Page 4; Column 1; View Desk, 451 words, INTO THE NIGHT: RSVP; SPIELBERG HONORED AT A-LIST BENEFIT EVENT, By BILL HIGGINS, SPECIAL TO THE TIMES

18.   Ladies Home Journal, October, 1994, Vol. 111; No. 10; Pg. 158; ISSN:
0023-7124, 1724 words, Kate Capshaw: loving Steven; actress and wife of director
Steven Spielberg; Interview, Gerosa, Melina, IAC 15847434

19.   South China Morning Post, September 28, 1994, FEATURE; Tv Eye; Pg. 24, 907
words, No Turkish delight, David Dalton

20.   Los Angeles Times, September 7, 1994, Wednesday, Home Edition, Life & Style;
Part E; Page 1; Column 1; View Desk, 1158 words, THE STARS COME OUT FOR CHILDREN;
HEALTH: THE HOLLYWOOD ELITE BEHIND THE CHILDREN'S ACTION NETWORK USES ITS CELEBRITY-
HOOD TO SPOTLIGHT THE PLIGHT OF KIDS., By PAMELA WARRICK, TIMES STAFF WRITER

21.   St. Louis Post-Dispatch, September 7, 1994, WEDNESDAY, FIVE STAR Edition,
NEWS; Pg. 1A, 1072 words, IN-STATE FUNDS BUOY ASHCROFT, NOT WHEAT; SENATE
CAMPAIGN CONTRIBUTION REPORTS ANALYZED, Kathleen Best Post-Dispatch Washington
Bureau, WASHINGTON

22.   The San Francisco Chronicle, AUGUST 28, 1994, SUNDAY, SUNDAY EDITION,
SUNDAY DATEBOOK; Pg. 26, 2733 words, SPOTLIGHT ON THE SEASON OCTOBER, Edward Guth-
mann, Jesse Hamlin, Joshua Kosman, Mic

23.   Newsday, August 15, 1994, Monday, CITY EDITION, NEWS; Pg. 12, 653 words,
INSIDE NEW YORK, By Michael Shain and Anthony Scaduto, COLUMN

That list gives you an idea of how powerful such a search can be. After
all, how else could you have found a story about Capshaw in the *South
China Morning Post?* Two stories, however, appear to be of particular interest—a *Ladies Home Journal* profile of Capshaw that focuses on her marriage
to Spielberg and a curious story in the *St. Louis Post-Dispatch* that appears
to focus on campaign contributions to Missouri Senate candidates. What
could that possibly have to do with Capshaw? A review of the article
shows it is a recap of political contributions to Senate candidates John
Ashcroft, the Republican winner, and Alan Wheat, the Democratic loser.*

                    Copyright 1994 St. Louis Post-Dispatch, Inc.
                         St. Louis Post-Dispatch

                    September 7, 1994, WEDNESDAY, FIVE STAR Edition

SECTION: NEWS; Pg. 1A

LENGTH: 1072 words

HEADLINE: IN-STATE FUNDS BUOY ASHCROFT, NOT WHEAT; SENATE CAMPAIGN CONTRIBUTION
REPORTS ANALYZED

BYLINE: Kathleen Best Post-Dispatch Washington Bureau

DATELINE: WASHINGTON

BODY:
   Missouri Senate candidates John Ashcroft and Alan Wheat are as much a study in
contrasts on the money trail as they are on the campaign trail, an analysis of their
donations shows.

*Reprinted with permission of the St. Louis Post-Dispatch, copyright 1994.

Fewer than half of the individuals giving money to Wheat, the Democrat, live in Missouri. Most of the individual donors to Ashcroft, the Republican, hail from the state. . . .

Wheat's donor list includes some of the biggest names in Hollywood. He collected $2,000—the maximum allowed for an individual—from film director Steven Spielberg; from Spielberg's wife, actress Kate Capshaw-Spielberg; and executives of Motown and Tabu Records.

You make a note to ask Capshaw about that donation. It is a way of delving into her personal views on politics and her life's philosophy. However, what really intrigues you is the *Ladies Home Journal* personality profile. It is exactly the kind of story you are planning. Some excerpts include the following:*

Copyright 1994 Information Access Co., a division of Ziff Communications Co.;
Copyright Meredith Corporation 1994
Ladies Home Journal

October, 1994

SECTION: Vol. 111 ; No. 10 ; Pg. 158; ISSN: 0023-7124

LENGTH: 1724 words

HEADLINE: Kate Capshaw: Loving Steven; actress and wife of director Steven Spielberg; Interview

BYLINE: Gerosa, Melina

BODY:
Quelle Barn (the name means "what a barn!), Steven Spielberg's multimillion-dollar compound in East Hampton, New York, is quite a distance from Ashland, Missouri, the town where Spielberg's wife, Kate Capshaw, worked as a grade school teacher. And now over a grilled chicken salad at The Honest Diner, a trendy Hampton eatery, Capshaw is savoring exactly how far she's come, literally and otherwise, from her native Midwest.

"I mean," she says in amazement, "I was a teacher of disabled children in a rural school district, where I sat in the lounge with the other teachers and drank Folgers coffee with Coffee-mate, smoked cigarettes and talked about our babies and the Holocaust mini-series that was on television." Her small blue eyes have a star-ling, power-drill effect." Then boom, slam, dunk, quick out cut! I'm sitting having an interview with the very women's magazine I bought every month to get recipes out of."

Well, the transition hasn't been quite as easy, or as fast, as Capshaw makes it sound. In fact, her passage from a divorced single from mom to the wife of the world's most powerful film director has been as difficult as it is remarkable. But if there is one trait that has kept her going, it is her bright-eyed determination. The commercials and soap-opera appearances that she fought for as a fledgling actress in New York led eventually to movie roles, including the breakout part of the blond screamer in Spielberg's 1984 hit Indiana Jones and the Temple of Doom.

And that part led to something else as well: a passionate affair that culminated in the breakup of Spielberg's marriage to Amy Irving and his union with Capshaw. . . .

*©1994 Meredith Corporation. Used with the permission of *Ladies' Home Journal* magazine.

"It takes good running shoes to keep up with Kate," says Spielberg. "She has an agenda of things to do, and every morning she wakes everybody up with an explosion of energy and leads us through the day. It's like Whistle While You Work,' starring Kate Capshaw." (Their children now include four-year-old
Sasha; two-year-old Sawyer; Theo, the six-year-old African-American foster child the Spielbergs adopted in 1989; nine-year-old Max, Spielberg's son with
Irving; and Jessica, Kate's seventeen-year-old daughter from her first marriage.)

Nowadays, when either of the Spielbergs talks about their marriage, there is no hint of the angst that preceded it.

Instead, Capshaw will happily tell you of her years running the
Spielberg home. "I put together a family," she says, and instantly corrects herself. "We put together a family. We had five children in three years, Judaism (she converted), circumcisions, braces, marriage." She pauses for a moment. "Not to mention divorce," she says, applying more Tabasco sauce. "I've been busy."

Now the forty-year-old actress is so secure in her home life that she's putting some of her energy back into her career. After a five-year hiatus,
Capshaw has three significant roles: This September she plays Jam Wood's levelheaded wife in the Showtime thriller Next Door; in October she appears as Warren Beatty's girlfriend in Love Affair, the remake of An Affair to Remember, and in her biggest role to date, she's the ex-district attorney wife of Sean Connery in the 1995 adventure drama Just Cause. . . .

That is just a small fraction of the lengthy *Ladies Home Journal* interview, but it shows how valuable a search of the commercial databases can be. Not every individual is as famous and well-covered as Capshaw, of course, and finding information about more obscure individuals can be a lot more difficult. That is an even better reason to use the commercial databases. Finding a precious tidbit of information about an obscure person can be like finding a needle in a haystack. The computer is ideally suited to help; it becomes your personal researcher.

USING BOOLEAN CONNECTORS

In doing the previous Capshaw searches, the author used what are known as *Boolean connectors* to limit the search. Most searchable databases use Boolean logic to find words. That is computerese, so do not worry about the strict definition. Just understand that Boolean connectors are a means of limiting your search so you do not have to sort through thousands or even millions of articles. Some of the Boolean connectors differ from system to system, which makes a detailed explanation of them virtually useless here. However, an understanding of the most common ones will help.

The universal connectors, used in almost every system, are AND, OR and NOT. A search for KATE AND CAPSHAW, for example, produces articles containing both the first and last names of the actress (or anyone else who happens to have the same name). If, however, you were searching for articles about someone named Alan Capshaw and did not want to be inundated with citations about Kate, you would enter ALAN CAP-SHAW NOT KATE. A search for articles about the death of Audrey Hepburn might be constructed this way to eliminate articles about Katherine Hepburn:

AUDREY HEPBURN NOT KATHERINE

The key to efficient database searching is constructing a solid search strategy. Mike McKean, chair of the broadcast news department at the University of Missouri, produced these tips for searching Dialog:

1. Choose the most narrow or specific database category that is likely to include the material for which you are searching.
2. Use the connectors: AND, OR, NOT. Examples:

   Hillary Clinton AND health care
   Blacks OR African-Americans
   Hillary Clinton NOT cookies

3. Use the wildcard character: *?* Examples:

   woman or *women* or *womyn* becomes *wom?n*
   corporate or *corporation* becomes *corporat?*

4. Do not use stop words: *a, an, by, from, is, of, or, not, the, to, with*
   Dialog will refuse to search for these words or will treat them as connectors.
5. Use proximity connectors to find words within a specified number of words from each other within the text: *(3w)* or *(3n)* (The 3 can be any number.) Examples:

   Goldilocks (2w) Three Bears produces
   Goldilocks and the Three Bears
   President (2n) Chrysler Corporation produces
   President of the Chrysler Corporation or
   Chrysler Corporation President

6. Use nesting, or the grouping of search terms with parentheses. Example:

   (TV OR radio OR media) AND (poll? NOT Clinton)

This search would locate documents that have either *TV* or *radio* or *media* in them and have the words *poll* or *polls* or *pollsters* or *polling* but not the word *Clinton*.

A look at some of the differences in Nexis/Lexis commands illustrates the tough chore facing the searcher who must switch from one service to another:

In Nexis/Lexis, the connectors are AND, OR, AND NOT rather than Dialog's AND, OR, NOT. So make it *Hillary Clinton AND NOT cookies.*

Similarly, the wildcard characters in Nexis/Lexis are the asterisk (*) and the exclamation point (!) in lieu of Dialog's question mark (?). Thus a search for *woman* or *women* or *womyn* becomes *wom*n.*

Learning those differences takes time and patience. For the novice learning to use more than one system, remembering when to use which commands is a frustrating experience. One useful device is to limit your search by date. If, for example, you expect to find hundreds of stories on Kate Capshaw, you might choose to look only at the more recent articles. Limiting your search in Nexis/Lexis would require commands such as the following:

AND DATE BEF
AND DATE IS
AND DATE AFT _____ AND DATE BEF _____

Some examples:

Clinton and date aft 8/1/1994
Clinton and date bef 1/1/1994
Clinton and date is 8/30/1994
Clinton and date aft 1/1/1994 and date bef 3/31/1991

Each service has other shortcuts, but learning them can be difficult. Nexis/Lexis, for example, relies on a series of dot commands to help the user perform certain functions. Some examples include the following:

Display

.fu = FULL full text of document
.kw = KWIC (key words in context) fifteen searchable words
.ci = CITE bibliographic reference for each document

Review

.np = next page
.fd = first document
.fp = first page
.pp = previous page
.nd = next document

To help users who have difficulty remembering obscure commands, Nexis/Lexis now has a Windows-based user interface that enables the user simply to click on the appropriate menu item to perform the function. Other services are providing similar interfaces. The differences among them, however, remain an obstacle to easy use.

MEAD DATA CENTRAL (NEXIS/LEXIS)

One of the most popular commercial database services in U.S. newsrooms is Mead Data Central's Nexis/Lexis (see Figure 4.1). The Lexis part of the service is used primarily by attorneys. It traces court cases at both the federal and state level, and thus becomes an invaluable service for attorneys seeking precedents to use in their pleas. While legal decisions

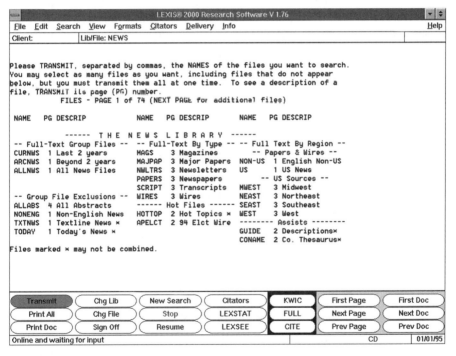

Figure 4.1   Lexis®-Nexis® is a character-based service, but a Windows interface with clickable menu bars makes it easier to navigate.

Reprinted with the permission of LEXIS-NEXIS, a division of Reed Elsevier Inc. LEXIS and NEXIS are registered trademarks of Reed Elsevier Properties, Inc.

often are useful to court reporters and other journalists, they are more likely to turn to Nexis, the service's news database.

Nexis contains the full text of many of the nation's leading newspapers and magazines. It also contains script material from numerous television outlets. A listing of some of those appears in Appendix A. Nexis/Lexis is thorough and complete, and journalists who use it regularly think they can no longer live without it.

For information contact Mead Data Central Inc., 9443 Springboro Place, P.O. Box 933, Dayton, OH 45401, tel. (800) 346–9759.

DIALOG

Dialog began as an abstract service, and as a result it contains the most comprehensive listings from magazines. In recent years it has increasingly added full-text services, which the market now demands. Nexis/Lexis took the early lead over Dialog in newsroom popularity because abstract services are not as useful to journalists; as noted earlier, there seldom is time to search out the original copy of a magazine in a library. As Dialog has added more and more full-text services, it has become increasingly attractive to newspapers, magazines and broadcast stations.

For information contact Dialog Information Services, 3640 Hillview Ave., Dept. 79, Palo Alto, CA 94304, tel. (800) 334–2564.

DATATIMES

DataTimes has its roots in the newspaper industry. It also contains the full text of many U.S. newspapers. Selecting Nexis or DataTimes often is a matter of which newspapers one would like to consult more frequently.

For information contact DataTimes, 14000 Quail Springs Highway, Suite 450, Oklahoma City, OK 73134, tel. (800) 642–2525.

DOW JONES

This service, as the name would suggest, is produced by Dow Jones and focuses on business data, including the full text of the *Wall Street Journal*. It is much more than that, however. It includes financial data from around the world, and its listing of data on corporations is invaluable. For news organizations that do a lot of business reporting, this service is a must.

For information contact Dow Jones, P.O. Box 300, Princeton, NJ 08543–0300, tel. (800) 522–3567.

BURRELLE'S BROADCAST DATABASE

Burrelle's Broadcast Database is a must for broadcast stations. It contains the transcripts of news and public affairs programs from three of the major networks, ABC, CBS and NBC, and selected programs from National Public Radio and others.

For information contact Burrelle's Broadcast Database, 75 E. Northfield Road, Livingston, NJ 07039, tel. (800) 631–1160.

NEWSNET

NewsNet is a database of more than five hundred newsletters and industry-specific reports. Worldwide wire services and stock quotes also are included. This is another great resource for business writers.

For information contact NewsNet, 945 Haverford Road, Bryn Mawr, PA 19010, tel. (800) 345–1301.

PRESSLINK

PressLink is perhaps the service that is most difficult to categorize. Its strength lies in graphics. Through PressLink, newspapers and magazines receive photos and information graphics from sources as diverse as Agence France-Presse, the Norwegian News Agency and the Knight-Ridder Graphics Network. However, it is more than a picture service. It contains several databases of interest to the industry, and it is a popular resting place for photographers on the information superhighway.

For information contact PressLink, 11800 Sunrise Valley Drive, Suite 1130, Reston, VA 22091, tel. (703) 758–1740.

WESTLAW

Like Nexis/Lexis, Westlaw contains records of court decisions and other legal matters. It can be of great use to court and government reporters.

For information contact Westlaw, 610 Opperman Drive, Eagan, MN 55123, tel. (800) 328–9352.

OTHER COMMERCIAL DATABASES

There are, of course, other commercial databases that may be of some use to journalists. These include Washington Alert, (800) 432–2250, Ext. 258, which allows the user to track bills in Congress; Super Bureau Inc., (800) 541–6821, a service that locates information for you and then transfers it to you by electronic mail; and MetroNet, (800) 927–2238, a service that helps locate people through a change-of-address database and the directory assistance files of the Bell Operating Companies.

5

EXPLORING THE INTERNET

Not long ago, the Internet was a place where only techies dared to tread. Its arcane Unix-based command structure was a huge deterrent to casual users. Even in the academic community, most did no more with the Internet than use it for electronic mail. Almost overnight, it seems, all that has changed.

Today, the Internet is arguably the most important library in the world, and it has become so easy to use that even the least technically oriented journalist should have no trouble navigating it. Indeed, those who are exposed to the Internet for the first time almost invariably become instantly addicted.

Why the sudden turnabout? Credit two institutions, The European Laboratory for Particle Physics in Switzerland (commonly known as CERN, the acronym for its French name) and the National Center for Supercomputing Applications (NCSA) at the University of Illinois. CERN invented the *World Wide Web* (WWW), a set of protocols for exchanging data, and *Hypertext Markup Language* (HTML), which permits the easy interchange and linking of documents. NCSA then developed Mosaic, a computer program that permits users to see HTML documents in a graphically pleasing form. The content does not stop with text-based documents. With Mosaic and HTML, it is easy to see photos and drawings, listen to sound or even play full-motion video clips.

With that capability suddenly available, commercial interest in the Internet began to blossom in 1994. Suddenly, the PIUs began a full-scale rush to see which could provide greater access to the Internet easier, cheaper and faster. Delphi was the early leader, but others were catching up quickly. Companies large and small suddenly saw the commercial potential of doing business on the Internet. Other companies rushed to provide the added security necessary to transact business in cyberspace, including, for example, the encryption of credit card data.

That latter issue highlights one of the remaining problems of the Internet. Security is still far from assured. Without encryption of data, it is possible for someone almost anywhere on the Internet (which includes practically every country in the world) to intercept data and use it illegally. Do not expect that to be a continuing hindrance to Internet commerce, however. Archrivals MasterCard and Visa have agreed on a joint encryption scheme that will permit secure credit card transactions on the Internet. It is merely a matter of time before the Internet carries massive amounts of commerce.

While the encryption problem is being worked out, companies by the thousands are rushing to create a presence on the Internet, if only as a means of hawking merchandise. Media companies are very much a part of that.

Time-Warner is a good example. That company has created an Internet site called *Pathfinder* (see Figure 5.1), which contains material from its various magazines, including TIME itself. Newspapers are into the act as well. Among the first with a presence on the Internet are the *Raleigh News and Observer* and the *Colorado Springs Gazette-Telegraph*. Both charge for access to their services, while so far Time-Warner's service remains free. Large and small newspapers in the United States and abroad are getting into the act. Titles on the Internet include the *St. Petersburg* (Russia) *Press*, the *San Francisco Examiner* and the *Digital Missourian*, an expanded version of the *Columbia* (Mo.) *Missourian*. Magazines on the Internet other than TIME include the *Washingtonian* and *Mother Jones*.

Perhaps because the Internet is still not an ideal place for doing business, free newspapers are most common there. College papers have taken the lead. Among the more innovative and attractive is the *Kansas State Electronic Collegian* (see Figure 5.2). Others include those published by the University of Queensland Department of Journalism and the University of Stockholm.

To view the Internet as merely a new mechanism for taking a printed publication and placing it online is a big, big mistake. The ability to include audio and video clips gives any such service an entirely new dimension. Many now view the Internet as the precursor to an entirely new medium, one with the potential of combining the best of newspapers and magazines with the best of television.

Consider this: Newspapers and magazines offer advantages that television cannot match. Those include portability and the space to carry large volumes of information. Those very characteristics have enabled

Figure 5.1 *Time* magazine maintains an impressive site on the World Wide Web.

Copyright Time Online. Reprinted by permission.

newspapers to fight off challenges from the broadcast media for large chunks of its advertising. Classified and coupon advertisements just do not work on television, nor do grocery advertisements, which contain lots of price information. Can you imagine someone reading a grocery ad on television?

However, the broadcast media, and television in particular, have strengths that newspapers cannot match. Television can transmit the news to consumers instantaneously, and it does so with sound and colorful visual appeal that newspapers and even magazines cannot equal. When something important happens in the world, the public turns to television first.

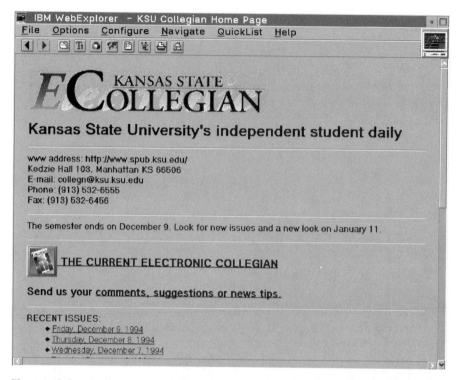

Figure 5.2 College newspapers have been leaders in moving their content onto the World Wide Web.

Reprinted with permission of *Kansas State Collegian*—Kansas State University.

What happens, though, if we suddenly create an electronically delivered news and information service that carries sound and video as well as text? What happens if we have a medium with virtually unlimited space and a printer attached to provide portability when needed? Such a medium combines the best of all the existing media into one very appealing package. The Internet does just that (see Figure 5.3). To be sure, it does it in rudimentary form; the sound and picture capability do not yet rival that of television.

That limitation, however, is largely a matter of bandwidth, or the pipe through which the information is delivered. Almost all connections to the Internet today are made through telephone lines, most of which are too limited to carry the amount of data necessary for a top-quality multimedia service. There is a rush to change that, led by the telephone and cable television companies.

Microsoft, the software behemoth, has joined with TCI, the nation's largest cable television operator, to explore ways of delivering a

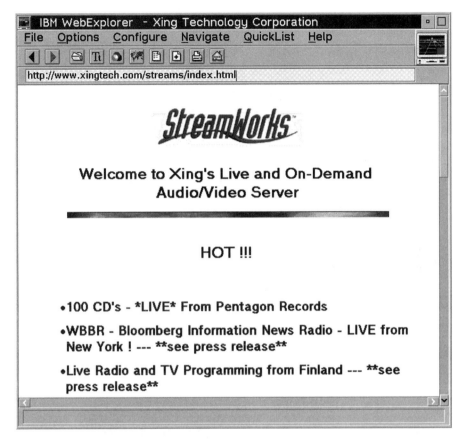

Figure 5.3   Xing's SteamWorks is one of the technologies that allows web site creators to include both audio and video on the Internet.

© Xing Technology Corporation, 1994–1996.

multimedia service into the home using cable television lines. Indeed, the Microsoft Network, mentioned as a newcomer in Chapter 3, may be those companies' attempt to bring this new medium to the home.

The Internet, though, is here today, and it contains a world of information that is free for the asking. Its underlying technology is being improved by the week, and anyone who tries to create a home-delivered information service will have to provide links to it. The Internet is, without a doubt, a big part of the media's future.

That means it is essential for the journalist to become well-acquainted with the Internet. The only way to do so is to explore it. This chapter can help. In it, we look at some of the terminology and technology you will need to understand. We also explore the various things you can find on the Internet. Finally, we take you on a tour of a couple of interesting sites for journalists.

LANGUAGE OF THE INTERNET

We already have encountered a few terms—World Wide Web, Mosaic and HTML—you will need to understand as you venture onto the Internet. As noted, WWW and Mosaic have made the Internet more user-friendly. Together, they have given the Internet a *graphical user interface* (GUI) that is easy to use. Underlying them is HTML, the markup language for documents that makes it all work.

Let us take a look at some other terms you will encounter. First, you will need some way to access the Internet, which will not be a problem if you work at a university, for the government or at one of the many companies that provide Internet access through their local computer networks. Even if your computer is connected to such a network, however, you will need some additional software. The most important is *TCP/IP*, which stands for Transmission Control Protocol/Internet Protocol. Think of it as a common transmission language for all computers on the Internet.

If you want access from home or from an office that is not connected to the Internet, you will have to contract for dial-up telephone service with an *Internet access provider.* Connections that allow you to use Mosaic or one of the other WWW *browsers* require a GUI (Windows, Macintosh or OS/2, most likely) and a fast modem (9600 baud is the absolute minimum). For access to the WWW, your provider also must have software called *SLIP* (Serial Line Internet Protocol) or *PPP* (Point-to-Point Protocol). You will need one of those on your computer, too. Without that capability, your Internet access will be severely restricted, so ask if SLIP or PPP is available. If you live in a large city, you should have no problem locating a provider. However, if you live in a rural area, chances are there is no local provider, which means you may have to pay long-distance charges to connect. That, of course, can be expensive.

Help is on the way. Several of the PIUs now provide fairly complete Internet access through their existing services, and most have toll-free numbers for those not in large metropolitan areas. Be aware, though, that some of the PIUs are struggling to provide full Internet access. Some claim to provide such access but merely allow users to send and receive electronic mail. Others add Usenet newsgroup access (which we will explain later). Some still do not allow WWW access, which is by far the easiest way to use the Internet. Further, be aware that home access to the Internet today can be costly. Expect to pay about $1 an hour just to be connected. That may not sound like much, but the charges add up in a hurry. If you subscribe to pay-for-use services, you can add to that figure.

If you know anything about the history of the Internet, you are probably asking: Why do I have to pay to use it? Wasn't the Internet established as a free service by the government? That is the popular perception, but of course nothing is really free. In the past, government created the Internet infrastructure with huge contributions from the Department of Defense and the National Science Foundation. Universities helped by paying for their connections to it. What resulted was a huge worldwide network. The federal government is in the process of sharply curtailing its contributions to the Internet, leaving future development to its users—universities, commercial operations and others. As a result, expect to see charges for more and more Internet services.

Home access to the Internet will require you to obtain TCP/IP software, a browser and other software to take full advantage of the Internet's services. All of that software can be obtained free from various Internet sites, and a friend who is already connected can help. As an alternative, you can purchase commercial versions of the necessary software from an access provider or a software vendor. The commercial versions often are easier to install and somewhat more robust than the freeware available on the Internet. Mosaic is a good example. You can obtain it free by download from NCSA, but companies that have licensed and improved the software offer more capable and more stable versions.

Indeed, Mosaic is now merely one of several Internet *browsers.* Others include Cello, Netscape, MacWeb for the Macintosh and its cousin, WinWeb for Microsoft Windows. IBM offers a rock-solid browser called WebExplorer for its increasingly popular OS/2 operating system, and versions for other platforms, including Windows, are promised. IBM became the first operating system vendor to bundle Internet access with its software when the company released OS/2 Warp, Version 3.0, in late 1994. The bundled software makes it easy for OS/2 users to dial in to Advantis, a worldwide dial-up telephone network service operated by IBM and Sears, and connect to the Internet instantaneously. Microsoft now offers the same with its Net Explorer packaged with Windows 95. When companies like that start providing easy access to the Internet, you know it is a hot item.

Once the connection is made, you will have to learn some other terminology. You will quickly have to learn about *URLs* (Uniform Resource Locators). Simply put, that is the address of a World Wide Web *home page* (front page) you can access with your browser. Unfortunately, URLs can be quite obscure. For example, the URL for NCSA home page at the University of Illinois is

http://www.ncsa.uiuc.edu/SDG/Software/Mosaic/
NCSAMosaicHome.html

The good news is that you will not have to remember that. Most browsers allow you to store that information with a click of the mouse. Returning to it then becomes a simple matter of clicking your mouse button on the related English equivalent from a list of frequently visited sites.

The HTML capability of WWW sites makes it easy for the user to use *hypertext,* a computer protocol that links one thing to another. When we read a book, we usually read it from front to back in linear fashion. With WWW documents, linear progression is not necessarily the best way to read. A highlighted word within the text, for example, means there is a hypertext link to something else. It may be a definition of the word, or it may be a related document. It may even be another publication on another WWW site in another country. Such is the power of hypertext. Links can be created that make a document—or a site—much more important than the sum of its contents. By pointing to related material throughout the World Wide Web, site creators are able to create links among related data no matter where they reside.

A good example is the *Digital Missourian,* which the author helped to create at the University of Missouri. The *Digital Missourian* (see Figure 5.4) has links to other news sites throughout the world. It is not necessary for the *DM* staff to update the weather daily. Because the *DM* has hypertext links to a wonderful weather site at the University of Illinois, users get hourly weather updates. Users who want basketball or football statistics for the Big Eight Conference get them through a link to Kansas State University, where they are updated weekly.

Publishing on the WWW, then, involves much more than creating your own material. The entire Internet in effect becomes your own wire service, capable of providing all sorts of data. The industry has merely begun to tap the power of that.

Now that we have learned about some of the terminology that surrounds the World Wide Web, let us look at some other terms frequently encountered on the Internet:

Archie—A search program for locating files stored on FTP servers (see definition later in this list).
Cyberspace—A term used to describe the entire world of online services.

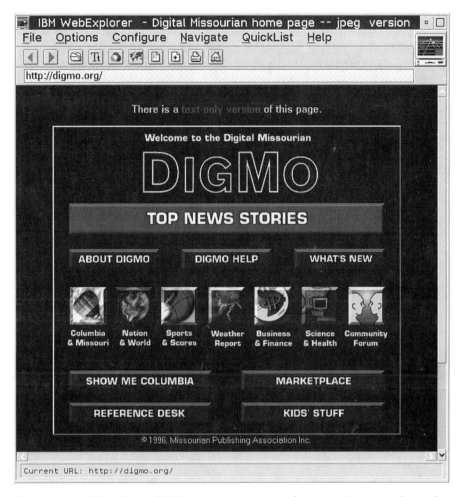

Figure 5.4 The Digital Missourian is one of a growing number of local newspapers with a significant presence on the World Wide Web.

©1996 Missourian Publishing Association Inc.

DNS—Domain Name System. A structure for translating numeric Internet addresses into strings of words denoting user names and locations.

Finger—Software used to determine whether another user is logged on to the Internet.

FTP—File Transfer Protocol. This protocol makes it possible to transfer files between a host computer and a remote one. It is used often to upload (transmit) or download (receive) software.

Gopher—A search tool developed at the University of Minnesota (whose mascot is the Golden Gopher). Before Mosaic and the WWW, Gopher was the best way to navigate the Internet, and it is still widely used. Gopher sites are accessible through most WWW browsers.

IRC—Internet Relay Chat. Software that allows keyboarded live discussions across the Internet.

Listserv—List Server. A listserv is a mailing list feature that enables users interested in a specific topic to send a message to all subscribers to the list without individual addressing. In most cases, you can subscribe to a listserv by sending an e-mail message to its address. In the body of the message, type *subscribe* (or *sub*) *carr-l [your name]*.

Newsgroup—A forum or conference area where you can post public messages and exchange ideas with others interested in a specific topic. There are thousands of such forums on Usenet, part of the Internet. Newsgroups can be of immense value to journalists searching for experts on a topic. Simply post a message and wait for the replies to roll in.

Ping—A TCP/IP utility that sends packets of information on the network. It is used to determine whether a computer is connected to the Internet.

SMTP—Simple Mail Transfer Protocol. A protocol that allows electronic mail to move from point to point on the Internet.

Telnet—A terminal emulation protocol that permits a user to log on to another computer on the Internet.

Usenet—User Network. A public network made up of thousands of discussion groups, called newsgroups. Newsgroups are organized by topic.

Veronica—Another search tool similar to Archie. It searches text that appears in Gopher menus.

WAIS—Wide Area Information Server. WAIS is software that indexes large text files in computer databases. Users use keywords to help locate material of interest.

Winsock—Windows Socket. An application programming interface (API) designed to allow Windows applications such as Mosaic to run over a TCP/IP network.

Those are the most common terms you are likely to encounter on the Internet. Some of these are programs that will complement TCP/IP, Winsock and the browser on your computer. Typically, programs such as Gopher, Telnet and Ping are placed in an Internet folder for use when you need them.

WHAT IS ON THE INTERNET?

First, understand that there is no way we can answer that question here. There is simply too much to list. It cannot even be done in those six-hundred-page manuals designed for that purpose. Of course, the Internet's growth is tremendous; each day of the year new sites are added on almost every conceivable topic. We have attempted to list in Appendix C the best-known sites on the Internet published by news companies—newspapers, magazines and broadcast stations. The list changes daily, so newer sites will not be listed there. Undoubtedly, some will die or move to other locations. Still, our list in Appendix C is a good place to start exploring.

The Internet has much more than just news, though. In general, the core of the Internet is information provided by two main sources—government agencies and universities. It is now possible to expand that to a third source—corporations.

Let us start with the federal government. Through the Internet, almost every government agency provides information to the public. That starts with the White House, which under Bill Clinton and Al Gore established a White House home page on the WWW. The Clinton administration also became the first to make it possible for the public to send electronic mail to the government's top leaders. You can write to the president by sending electronic mail to:

president@whitehouse.gov

Incidentally, that is a fairly typical e-mail address. You can write to the author by sending mail to:

jourbsb@muccmail.missouri.edu

The last field in each address lets you know the primary domain of the individual user. In the president's case, he can be found at *gov*, the government domain, while the author is at *edu*, an educational site. Commercial users can be found at *com* sites, and military users at *mil* sites. Outside the United States, a two-letter country code is used for the domain—*es* for Spain, *lv* for Latvia, and so on. Missouri is the address for everyone at the University of Missouri, and the rest is locally designated for traffic-keeping purposes.

The White House home page is a fascinating site. Indeed, it may be one of the most interesting on the WWW. Once there, you can take a tour of the White House (through viewing excellent photos of all its rooms) and listen to a recorded message from the president (if your computer has sound capability).

Other government agencies have sites that almost certainly are more useful to journalists. It is possible, for example, to check the census data of any city or county in the country. Once there, you can determine the racial breakdown of the community, its economic vitality and similar items. That can be invaluable information for a reporter. It is also possible to check the maintenance records of all aircraft registered in the United States. When a plane crash occurs in your area, it becomes an easy chore to check its record.

You also can read press releases from almost every government agency, review calls for grant proposals or check servers set up by the House and Senate. NASA also has several sites of interest. The Department of Agriculture includes crop data, and there is even a site for the U.S. Military Academy.

Can any journalist afford not to be acquainted with such material? Today, that is unimaginable.

States are hopping on the bandwagon, too, although some are far ahead of others. Many of the low-tax states lag badly in making information available to the public this way. Still, even in those states the universities provide plenty of material of interest. In Missouri, for example, you can access some material through the state government, but the University of Missouri has some invaluable databases of interest to journalists. These include a database of all licensed drivers in the state. Washington University in St. Louis also provides excellent resources on the Internet.

Some cities and counties are on the Internet, too. A leader in this area is Cleveland, which is the best-known of the so-called *freenet* sites. Freenets were set up to provide community information and to offer text-based links to the Internet. A few are adding WWW access. In communities with freenets, users can get a password at no cost. Armed with a computer, a modem and that password, the Internet is available, although most often in character mode only. Typically, freenets are sponsored by local governments and universities in the area. Sometimes, local libraries are involved.

Universities, of course, are a major contributor to the Internet. Without exploring on your own, you cannot begin to understand the wealth of information they make available to users throughout the world. Washington University maintains one of the largest and best repositories of computer software in the world. Anyone on the Internet can access it with an anonymous FTP.

Interested in obtaining a copy of the Estonian constitution? It's easy to do on the Internet, thanks to a site maintained in Tallinn, that country's capital. In a matter of seconds, you can access data on the Great Barrier Reef directly from Australia.

As the Internet becomes increasingly commercialized, material posted by companies is becoming more and more important. Already, information is available on thousands of products and services. Some companies are posting useful databases as a means of teasing the sales of access to more comprehensive services, and yes, it is already possible to buy things there, including the latest books about Internet services.

Earlier, we referred to the Internet as the world's largest library. That is exactly what it is, and no journalist can do without it.

SITES FOR JOURNALISTS

One of the strengths of the Internet is the ability to link one site to many. That makes it possible to access all of the Internet's resources on a topic of interest. Someone, of course, has to do the work to make that happen. Two excellent web sites attempt to help journalists by compiling links to other useful sites. These can be found at:

http://www.missouri.edu/~jschool/hotlinks/index.html

and

http://www.jou.ufl.edu/commres/jouwww.htm

The first is a listing of resources useful to journalists compiled by Kate Akers, a staff member at the University of Missouri. The second is a list of college and university journalism resources compiled by journalists at the University of Florida.

Another useful site for locating news organizations on the World Wide Web is NewsLink (see Figure 5.5). NewsLink's URL is:

http://www.newslink.org/

All those sites provide links to extremely useful resources. Because of that, they serve as excellent starting points for the journalist exploring the Internet for the first time. Even for experienced Internet users, the links remain useful.

Several listservs of interest to journalists also exist on the Internet. Because listservs are based on electronic mail, anyone on the Internet can subscribe, and World Wide Web capability is not needed. The most popular listservs for journalists are

- Computer-Assisted Reporting and Research. To subscribe, send a subscription message to *carr-l@ulkyvm.louisville.edu.*
- The Center for Investigative Reporting. To subscribe, contact *cir@igc.apc.org.*
- Copy Editing. Contact *copyediting-l@cornell.edu.*
- Investigative Reporters and Editors. Contact *http://www.ire.org.*

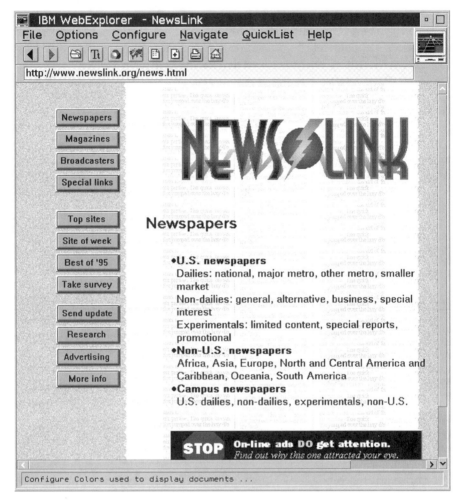

Figure 5.5 NewsLink provides an excellent service to help web users locate media sites online.

Reprinted with permission of NewsLink Associates.

- National Institute for Computer-Assisted Reporting. Contact *http://www.nicar.org.*
- MIT Media Lab. Contact *online-world@media-lab.mit.edu.* The Media Lab also has a World Wide Web site at *http://www.media.mit.edu.*

Finally, there are several Usenet Newsgroups of interest to journalists. These include *alt.journalism, alt.journalism.criticism, alt.politics.media* and *alt.news.media.* There you will find many journalists and those eager to criticize them.

6

ADVANCED DATABASE
TECHNIQUES

Ida Tarbell would love it. That pioneering investigative reporter helped set the standard for investigative reporting in the early 20th century with her disclosures about the stranglehold of Standard Oil's monopoly. Like Tarbell, today's investigative reporters have to pound the pavement and talk with hundreds of sources to produce a major story. However, today's reporters have a tool that Tarbell did not have and could not even dream about—the computer. Consider these recent examples of computer-assisted reporting:

- The *Miami Herald,* during its coverage of Hurricane Andrew, discovered that lax building codes contributed significantly to the devastation and documented that fact.
- The *Kansas City Star's* Jeff Taylor and Mike McGraw showed the U.S. Department of Agriculture to be undermined by fraud, waste and favoritism toward powerful food lobbies.
- The *Indianapolis Star's* Joseph Hallinan and Susan Headden revealed a pattern of extensive medical malpractice in Indiana.
- The Minneapolis *Star Tribune's* Lou Kilzer and Chris Ison uncovered an arson scheme in nearby St. Paul that involved firefighters.
- The *Atlanta Journal and Constitution's* Bill Dedman exposed racism in mortgage lending by Atlanta banks and savings and loans.[1]

What all those stories have in common is that they won Pulitzer Prizes, and they all were done with the considerable help of computers.

Plenty of stories that do not win Pulitzers are being done with the help of computers these days, too. Explains Elliot Jaspin, a Pulitzer winner himself and systems editor for Cox Newspapers in Washington: "What's happened over the last 10 years is that the government has increasingly used computers to manage its operations, so there's been an enormous transfer of data to electronic form. . . . You need a computer to get at it."[2]

More and more journalists are learning how to do just that. Investigative Reporters and Editors, the national trade association for investigative journalism, has helped. IRE and a related unit, the National Institute for Computer-Assisted Reporting (NICAR), tour the country giving week-long seminars to working journalists on the skills required for computer-assisted reporting. It is a retraining effort for those who went through journalism schools before such techniques were common. A Freedom Forum study found that computer and database skills ranked fourth—behind writing, reporting and editing—among skills that journalists most wanted to develop.[3]

Much of NICAR's training effort revolves around how to get the data you need and how to process it into something meaningful. Most government data are stored on nine-track mainframe data tapes that probably contain a lot more facts than the reporter needs. The trick is to extract the pertinent data and then determine what they tell you (see Figure 6.1). That is not an easy chore in itself, but some stories require even more work—comparing one database to another. That is when it is time for the reporter to learn about *relational databases.*

Say, for example, that you have extracted from a government database of driver's license records a list of all the school bus drivers in your state. You also have extracted from court records a list of all those convicted of drunken driving in the last three years. With a relational database, you can compare the two and determine how many school bus drivers have DWI convictions over that time span. Great stuff.

Of course, there is plenty of reporting left to do after the data are in hand. You will have to look for particular areas of the state where the problem is worst, interview school officials to determine whether the problem was known to them and interview parents of children affected. You will probably want to interview the drivers as well.

Ever since Ida Tarbell's day, journalists have claimed to be the public's watchdogs over the conduct of government. The ability to do computer-assisted reporting has raised the level of such reporting to new heights. It also has created a need for journalists better-trained to cope with the demands of a profession that is suddenly more heavily driven by technology.

Figure 6.1 The National Institute of Computer-Assisted Reporting helps train reporters in extracting data from nine-track mainframe tapes.

GETTING ACCESS TO DATA

The federal Freedom of Information Act and state *sunshine laws,* or open meetings and records laws, have made it easier to win access to the government data necessary to do such reporting. However, access is far from certain, and government officials often try to create insurmountable hurdles to reporter access. When the *Houston Chronicle* asked the Texas Department of Public Safety for a computer database containing the names of the state's 12.5 million licensed drivers, the department replied it would be happy to help—just as soon as the newspaper produced $60 million. That was based on the department's statutory authority to charge $6 each for the first 100 records and $5 a record for the remainder.[4]

What the *Chronicle* wanted was a computer tape of the records, but the department demanded payment based on an old law that dealt with paper records. Paper records, of course, are more costly to produce. Duplicating the state's computer tape would result in minimal time and materials costs. Its mainframe could easily generate a duplicate tape overnight. Even when laws prohibit the release of some information in the database, such as juvenile records, a simple programming change can produce a tape that eliminates those records before the duplicate is handed over to reporters.

Unfortunately, though, incidents such as the one in Texas still occur frequently. In part, that is because many states have not yet modified their laws to take into account the ease of access that computers allow. Officials use those outdated laws to limit access to the information. Sometimes that is because they are trying to hide embarrassing information. Sometimes they are simply tempted by the revenue that excessive charges could bring to their offices.

Sandra Davidson, an attorney and journalism professor, argues that a good law for access to computerized public information should have 12 elements:*

- A definition of *public records* that is broad enough to include computerized records.
- A presumption that information collected by government is open to the press and public.
- The inclusion of redactional language, which allows officials to edit out restricted information before data are released. Without that, such restrictions become an excuse to withhold information.
- Assurances of access for all citizens regardless of the purpose for which information is sought.
- Cost containment that allows records to be reproduced (1) for the cost of staff time and actual duplication and (2) with a waiver of costs when the information is to be used for the purpose of informing the public. Vague language calling for *reasonable* or *actual* costs often proves to be inadequate.
- Language that permits appropriate tailoring. In other words, when a requester wants information in a specific form, and if a computer system can produce information in that form, then the requester should be able to get it in that form.
- A requirement that custodians of records keep information in a form that is easily retrievable.
- Time limits that prevent custodians from dragging their feet in producing public records.
- Language that creates a state board or agency to provide the computer expertise that custodians of records need.
- Language that creates mandatory instructions to custodians on the proper maintenance and storage of computer records.

*Reprinted with permission of Sandra Davidson (Scott).

- Language that creates mandatory instructions regulating the destruction of records.
- Provisions for sanctions against custodians who fail to follow statutes on access to information.[5]

Thanks to a lot of work by the media, professional journalism organizations, journalism schools, public-watchdog organizations and a few politicians who really believe that the public's business should be made public, much progress has been made in winning access to information. However, problems with access are not likely to disappear for at least two reasons:

- There is mounting concern that easy access to things like driver's license records will help criminals find people they seek to harm. Indeed, in at least one instance a California murder investigation revealed that the murderer located his victim that way.
- There is concern in some quarters that public records will be misused by marketers. It would be easy, for example, for a company selling diet products to produce a mailing to overweight drivers, identified by plucking their weights from driver's license records.

Supporters of free access to public information insist that there are ways to prevent those undesirable side effects while protecting the public's right to know. Most journalists argue for the maximum amount of disclosure. In a free society, that principle is fundamental.

ANALYZING THE DATA

Once you have obtained a nine-track data tape, your work as a reporter has just begun. Now it is time to see what you have. Unfortunately, that is not as simple as turning on your personal computer.

For one thing, most personal computers are not set up to read mainframe tapes, and most newspapers do not have mainframes on which to process them either. That means you will need to invest in some equipment. The most common way to access mainframe data is to purchase a nine-track tape drive. Using an adapter card, the external device can be connected to your PC.

Then, you will need to be able to read the tape in the format in which it is written. It will help if the agency from which you obtained it provides a list of the data fields included. If not, you will need a utility program that identifies those fields for you by reading a sample from the tape. Once you see what is there, you will need to decide which fields are worth saving and which can be discarded. You will want to rid yourself of unneeded data. Failure to do so may well make the size of your database unmanageable on a PC. Remember, it was created on a mainframe, and a database of something like driver's license records is huge, even for a small state.

Once you have decided on the fields to be retrieved, with the help of some good software it is a matter of letting the computer extract the data from the nine-track tape. It will build a new, smaller database for your PC. If your project involves a comparison with data from two or more databases, you will have to process them all before you are ready to proceed.

Database software comes in two flavors, *flat file* and *relational*. Flat-file databases are fine for maintaining simple address books, but for this kind of work, you will need a relational database such as Microsoft FoxPro. That has become an increasingly popular standard for journalists.

Obviously, such work should not be done by novices. One simple mistake in extracting data or in interpreting results can distort the results of the whole study. That is why a working knowledge of statistics is important and why many top journalism schools now require statistics courses for graduation. Bob Mitchell, an investigative reporter for Thomson Newspapers, discussed problems he encountered while dealing with a tape of political contributions provided by the Federal Election Commission:

> *High technology creates the impression of infallibility, but numbers spewing from a printer or flashing across a computer screen are not guaranteed to be error-free.*
>
> *Two problems often arise. An FEC worker's input error might, for example, turn a $500 contribution into a $5,000 contribution. Another problem is the computer's need for specificity. Contributions from one person can often come from different locations, but computer database programs may not sort them together because they have different zip codes or towns in the address.*[6]

So despite its allure, computer-assisted reporting is no panacea. Databases do not produce good stories by themselves. As *Forum* magazine put it, "Computer-assisted reporting is still reporting, and sound journalism practices apply." Adds Penny Loeb, an associate editor at *U.S. News & World Report,* "I always spot-check. I'm always thinking what could go wrong."[7]

While a reporter at *New York Newsday* in 1991, Loeb used computers to reveal that New York City property owners were not notified about $275 million in taxes they had overpaid. No story of that type would have been possible without a helping hand from the computer; it would have taken Loeb several lifetimes to track down those records by hand. Still, to complete the story plenty of reporting was required. All the while, Loeb kept asking herself what could be wrong with the data.

Such caution is both enviable and essential. Notes Elliot Jaspin of Cox Newspapers, "Computers don't make a bad reporter into a good reporter. What they do is make a good reporter better. What they allow a bad reporter to do is make bigger mistakes faster."

DEBUNKING SOME MYTHS

Most discussions of computer-assisted reporting center around the spectacular, Pulitzer-winning investigative articles. Those are glamourous, to be sure, but increasingly computer-assisted journalism is making its way into the mainstream. No longer are computers the exclusive province of investigative reporters. Notes Atlanta's Bill Dedman, "Let's say you hear that Jesse Jackson is running for mayor of Washington. Does he own property in the District of Columbia? The records office has been closed for three hours, but you can find out because your computer can access the database. Or there's a shooting. Does the person have a gun permit? A store goes out of business. Has the owner filed for bankruptcy?"[8]

Journalists who know how to use computers can find the answers quickly and easily, particularly if they have links to government databases, as some now do.

Another myth about computer-assisted reporting is that it is expensive. However, a newspaper can set up an excellent system to analyze nine-track tapes for about $6,000. Additionally, the purchase of tapes from government agencies, if properly negotiated, can be quite reasonable. Even the smallest newspaper, magazine or broadcast station should be able to afford that.

Nor is computer-assisted reporting difficult to learn. Many who have taken NICAR's week-long seminar have gone on to do published investigations with no additional training. Further, NICAR's staff is always there to help. Finally, more and more journalism schools are adding courses in computer-assisted reporting to their curricula. In many cases, learning to be productive with your computer is as simple as taking such a class.

ENDNOTES

1. *The Forum,* September 1993, p. 7.
2. Ibid, p. 4.
3. Ibid, p. 5.
4. *Editor & Publisher,* March 5, 1994, p. 17.
5. *Editor & Publisher,* Nov. 2, 1991, pp. 8–13pc.
6. Handout prepared for IRE Conference in St. Louis, July 1994.
7. *The Forum,* September 1993, p. 6.
8. Ibid.

7

CREATING YOUR OWN DATABASES

Unfortunately, not every database a journalist needs can be found in the PIUs, in commercial databases or on the Internet. Sometimes pertinent databases just do not exist, and sometimes public officials block access to them. That is when it is time to consider creating your own database. If numbers are involved, the task may call for a spreadsheet.

The challenge comes in selecting the program to use; not all computer programs are created equally, and matching your task to the appropriate program can save plenty of time and anguish. It helps, then, for today's reporter or editor to be computer-literate. Journalism is no longer a field in which one can work without learning the ins and outs of computing.

That is increasingly true as newspapers, magazines and broadcast stations abandon their old minicomputer- or mainframe-based computer systems in favor of personal computer networks. Unlike the dedicated terminals used in older systems, personal computers make it possible to take advantage of thousands of off-the-shelf software products. Good computer tools can simplify your job, but they can do so only if you make the effort to learn what programs are available and how to use them. Once you have learned what tools you need, insist that your employer provide them. Unfortunately, some publications and broadcast stations are so far behind in providing such tools that it may be necessary to strike out on your own.

CHOOSING YOUR TOOLS

The first step is to take an inventory of the kinds of things you do as a reporter or editor and start looking for programs that can help. If you are like most journalists, the tools for your computer desktop should include the following:

- *The usual complement of a word processor, electronic mail, access to your morgue, access to the PIUs and commercial databases, and access to online versions of dictionaries, thesauruses and stylebooks.*
- *A notepad.* These simplified word processors are useful for taking notes while on the telephone. Why take notes with paper and pencil when later on you will want to move those quotes onto the computer anyway? Your word processor will work just as well, although some reporters prefer notepads because they are smaller programs and load into the computer's memory more quickly.
- *A calculator.* Reporters have to deal with math frequently. A calculator on your computer desktop can make that a snap.
- *A spreadsheet.* More advanced computational problems require a spreadsheet. A good spreadsheet such as Microsoft Excel or Lotus 1-2-3 is essential for today's business reporter; spreadsheets can help spot trends in revenues and expenses in corporate annual reports that otherwise would be difficult to notice. Similarly, government reporters, who must deal with budgets and audits, can make great use of a spreadsheet's rich mathematical abilities. Further, spreadsheets allow you to produce simple charts and graphs from the data, which makes it easier to spot trends. So much of today's reporting centers on money and finance that it is difficult to imagine any reporter who could not benefit from a working acquaintance with spreadsheet software.
- *A charting and graphing program.* At most newspapers, magazines and broadcast stations, there are graphic artists to produce such charts for you. However, in many cases it will help if you provide a rough first effort. To do so, you will need access to a charting program (see Figure 7.1). If you have a spreadsheet, its simple built-in charting program may suffice.

More and more reporters are using such tools not only at the office but also on the road. Today's laptop, notebook and palmtop computers are productive tools for the well-trained journalist. With the proper hardware and software tools in place, the journalist of the Information Age is well-equipped to perform.

CHOOSING THE RIGHT DATABASE

Because there are so many types of database programs designed for so many different purposes, let us do a quick review of the most common types and their intended uses.

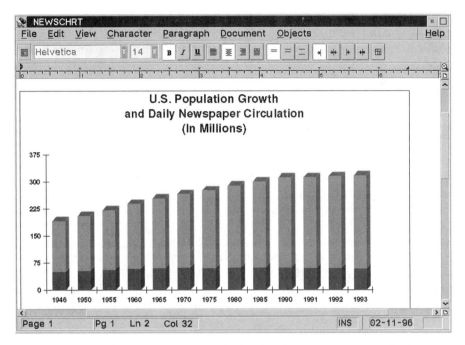

Figure 7.1   A charting program helps both reporters and their readers get a grasp on complicated sets of numbers.

Simple problems require simple answers. Reporters typically build up a huge list of sources, and a program to help keep track of telephone numbers can be useful. For that purpose, a simple, multipurpose *flat-file database* will suffice, but a *personal information manager* (PIM), in reality a specialized form of the flat-file database, is ideally suited. Keeping up with phone numbers is such a common business problem that hundreds of such programs exist. Any computer store salesperson can help. If you are a heavy user of personal computers, you might want to choose one that dials numbers for you through your modem.

Similarly, off-the-shelf *calendar databases* can be of great use to reporters and editors, who must manage their time well to remain efficient. There is nothing worse than being late for a meeting with an important source—except forgetting about the meeting altogether. Such programs often are an integral component of PIMs.

More complex problems require other solutions. Some reporters—especially investigative reporters—often have problems keeping up with and organizing their notes. For a major investigation, a reporter (or a team of reporters) might compile hundreds of notebooks worth of notes. When it is time to write the story, sorting through the mound of information can be a real headache. A popular program for solving that problem is AskSam, a *full-text database* that allows you to organize and index free-form text such as notes and quotes. It has become well-known to investigative reporters.

Larger and more complex projects will require a more powerful full-text database. One terrific tool for indexing large amounts of text is a program called *Folio,* an indexing engine used in some newspaper library systems. Once material is indexed in a Folio infobase, full-text searches of the database are possible. This may prove useful for indexing large amounts of material obtained on nine-track tape or downloaded from external sources. If you have such a need, check with your librarian or computer support staff; your newspaper may already have the program in-house.

Relational database work, as we learned in Chapter 6, requires a more sophisticated database such as Microsoft's FoxPro or Borland's Paradox. Smaller jobs are handled well by Microsoft Access, which some consider easier to use than FoxPro or Paradox. Other popular programs for relational work include network-based products such as Oracle, Btrieve and DB2/2. Mainframes are well-suited to such tasks if one is available.

THE BASICS OF DATABASES

Other than full-text databases, most database programs rely on fields of fixed width into which the user enters data. So, before you can put data into a file, you must define its structure. That involves giving each field a name, designating the type of content it will contain (characters, numbers, dates, memos, or simple yes-no or true-false responses) and specifying the width of the field.

The strength of databases lies in their ability to quickly sort the data you have entered. In effect, you are telling the program to perform a simple *find* command—find all the people in the database who live in Tennessee, find all the people with the last name of Brown or find all who work as plumbers. Once data are stored, it becomes a simple matter to sort them—or find things—using any of the entered fields.

A key to success is making sure that the field structure is adequate for your intended use. It is possible to add fields later, or modify the widths of fields, with most database programs. However, doing so can be time-consuming, and it is a time-saver to do it right the first time.

This simple example shows why:

Let us say you are creating an address list that contains the common two-letter U.S. Postal Service abbreviations for states. You know that field will remain constant in width, so you can save a lot of time by making it exactly two characters wide. When you have entered the state, the program will automatically take your cursor to the next field. If your field is too long, you will have to strike the TAB or ENTER key to go to the next field, which will result in an added step for each address you enter. If you are entering hundreds of addresses, that can be time-consuming.

As we learned in Chapter 6, relational databases add the ability to compare one database with another. It is important to choose the right tool for the job at hand. It would make little sense to enter data into a database without relational capability if the job will require that level of sophistication. On the other hand, it might be overkill to create a simple address-book application in one of the complex relational database programs. Choosing the right tool is as important for the reporter or editor as it is for the carpenter.

THE BASICS OF SPREADSHEETS

Today's best database programs have excellent mathematics capabilities, and today's best spreadsheets are quite adequate for simple database work. As programs have become more and more sophisticated, the distinction between the two has blurred. Still, it is fair to say that spreadsheets are maximized for mathematical functions whereas databases are maximized for storing and sorting text. Again, it is important to choose the best tool for the job.

A good spreadsheet program will allow much more flexibility than a database program in linking one spreadsheet to another. For example, you might want to construct spreadsheets of spending for various city departments and link them to a master spreadsheet that shows all city expenditures. Doing that with a database program would be difficult if not impossible. Further, a good spreadsheet will have graphing and charting capability you are unlikely to find in a database program. Sometimes the best way to spot changes in a company's income or expenses is to chart the data. Charts will help illustrate things in ways that numbers on a page never can. With that capability, reporters and editors also can provide simple charts and graphs to help a graphics artist do a better job.

In many ways, spreadsheets are more difficult to learn than database programs, and the concepts are more difficult to grasp. Using them requires at least a basic understanding of math, and journalists are notorious for their dislike of that subject. However, journalists are unlikely to make use of a spreadsheet's more advanced capabilities, including trigonometric or even statistical functions. If that is required, so is expert help. Instead, journalists must learn to use the more basic functions of spreadsheets, including how to write the mathematical formulas that make spreadsheets perform their computational wizardry (see Figure 7.2).

Like databases, spreadsheets are based on fields with certain widths and characteristics. In spreadsheets, however, each entry within a field is considered as a separate *cell*. That makes it possible, using formulas, to construct extremely sophisticated relationships among various cells. So, the characteristics of cells include not only width but also the row and column that give the cell its name. Cell B23, for example, would become the 23rd entry in Column B within the spreadsheet.

Cells also have attributes, such as *type* (blank, label or value), *status* (protected or unprotected, changeable or unchangeable), and *format* (dollar amounts, for example, might have two decimal points).

Spreadsheets are far too complex to explain in detail here, and the way they work varies a great deal. Once you have obtained a spreadsheet program, you will have to invest some time in learning to use it. Almost certainly, your choice will be one of the two market leaders, Microsoft

	BalanceSheet								▫ ☐
File	Edit	View	Character	Cell	Options	Chart			Help

▦ Swiss	⌄ 8	⌄	**B**	*I*	<u>U</u>	▤ ▤ ▤	Σ	▦ ▦

K11	= + − * / $$ ✓ ✗	=sum(K7:K10)

	F	G	H	I	J	K	L	↕
1		Quarterly Financial Statement for the period ending December 31, 1995						
2								
3		Balance Sheet						
4								
5		Assets						
6			Current assets					
7				Cash		$50,000		
8				Accounts Receivable		175,000		
9				Securities		65,000		
10				Inventory		575,000		
11				Total current assets		$865,000		
12			Fixed assets					
13				Vehicles		$250,000		
14				Equipment		750,000		
15				Land & buildings		1,500,000		
16				Subtotal		2,500,000		
17				Less accumulated depreciation		(1,250,000)		
18				Total fixed assets		$1,250,000		
19			Total assets			$2,115,000		

READY	Formula	02-11-9ϵ

Figure 7.2 Spreadsheets help reporters understand complex numbers. To use one, a reporter must learn how to enter basic formulas.

Excel or Lotus 1-2-3. Choosing which to use is a matter of preference and of having someone available who can help you learn to use one or the other. Increasingly, high schools and colleges are offering basic computer science courses that include the use of spreadsheets. Night courses, offered in most cities of any size, are another possibility.

One thing is clear: It is time for every reporter and editor to be conversant in the use of both databases and spreadsheets. The reporter or editor who does not use them sooner or later will spend time eating the dust of a competitor who does. Today, it is a matter of learn or be left behind.

AN EXAMPLE OF SUCCESS

Ralph Frammolino of the *Los Angeles Times* became a big believer in the power of creating databases only a couple of days after completing a NICAR training course on computer-assisted reporting. The judge and attorneys were close to making the first cut in the jury pool for the O.J. Simpson murder trial, and Frammolino's editor wanted a quick profile of those still in the running. Frammolino was handed a sheaf of three-page questionnaires completed by prospective jurors in the trial of Simpson, the Hall of Fame running back and television commentator. "Under normal circumstances," Frammolino wrote in *Uplink,* NICAR's newsletter, "we'd either eyeball the responses or tally up a few categories—race, sex, educational background—and paint a broad-brush portrait of the panel."[1]

This time, using Microsoft Access, Frammolino was able to do much more. "I decided to create about 30 fields to capture each juror's age, race, sex, educational level and home city, as well as key responses about media exposure, attitudes and personal habits that could be represented by symbols or a simple yes or no." Using that technique, he was able to record such things as whether the prospective juror watched the chase of Simpson's white Bronco on television and whether the juror had knowledge of an earlier Nicole Brown Simpson 911 call to police alleging domestic abuse by O.J.

Using Access, Frammolino sorted the database into two files—those who made the cut and those who did not—and kept adjusting those files constantly as the judge and attorneys made their decisions. By deadline, among other things, the *Times* was able to report in its summary of the remaining jury pool that 19 percent had experienced domestic violence.

The next day, a more difficult analysis compared those eliminated as prospective jurors with those retained. Each prospective juror had been asked to express an opinion about the reliability of DNA testing, a key piece of the evidence against Simpson. The numbers showed that 39 percent of those excused were likely to believe in the reliability of DNA testing compared to only 10 percent of those left in the jury pool. Combined with quotes from expert jury consultants, the *Times* had a terrific story that no other news medium could match.[2]

Such a story would have been tough, if not impossible, to do without computers. Equally impressive, it was done on deadline; it was not based on a drawn-out investigation.

ENDNOTES

1. Ralph Frammolino, *Uplink,* newsletter of the National Institute for Computer-Assisted Reporting, December 1994, p. 1.
2. Ibid, p. 4.

8

LEGAL ISSUES AND
THE ONLINE WORLD

Without a doubt, the most pressing legal issues facing the online world and journalists are those of copyright and government regulation. In the first case, online content providers are forced to work with copyright laws written with the printed word, not cyberspace, in mind. In the second, creators of the new media are forced to deal with the uncertainties of government regulation (or deregulation). Both are difficult issues, but other legal issues cloud the future, too. Let us examine the most important as they pertain to journalists.

COPYRIGHT AND ONLINE SERVICES

Lance Rose, an attorney and the author of *SysLaw,* describes the copyright problem clearly in an article in *Wired* magazine. Writes Rose, "What can copyright possibly mean when millions of people can download the information they find on the Internet? So far, the idea of open access to these materials hasn't slowed down the onslaught of new information flowing into the Net. But will information suppliers rebel against the status quo at some point? If they do clamp down, will the copyright laws be any help?"[1]
Rose concludes that there are four widely divergent ways of approaching those questions, ranging from no regulation at all to tightly written copyright laws. The options include the following:

- *There should be no copyright on network materials at all.* Those who argue for this position claim the Net is a shared public resource, and its riches should be available to all. However, as Rose notes, "What about the 'legal rule' that a copyrighted work is not available at all unless expressly placed in the public domain by the owner? Merely uploading a text onto the Net can't be a dedication to the public domain, unless we're ready to discourage authors of books and articles from placing their works on the Net. And what if copyrighted materials are placed on the Net without the owner's permission? Should the owner be able to sue for copyright infringement? Are copyrights somehow stripped off on the way into the Net, leaving the materials bare of legal protection?"

- *It is okay to quote from material on the Net without permission.* Rose observes that many journalists pick up material from the Net and quote it at will. There is a common myth that you can reproduce text or statements as long as you credit the author. In reality, you need permission unless there is a legal exception such as fair use. Asks Rose, "Will the look and feel of the Net—which some see as a collection of uncopyrightable discussions—somehow lead to a new 'legal rule' that permits rampant appropriation of others' online writings under the guise of quoting?"

- *Republishing of works taken from the Net is covered by the fair-use rule.* This rule, which allows very limited reproduction of minor excerpts, was intended to apply to educational uses and critical commentary. Rose notes that some bulletin board operators regularly publish CD-ROMs of BBS-resident shareware without obtaining the authors' permission. He also notes that computer artists have been known to plunder digitized images without permission. Rose asks, "Will fair use on the Net expand in the direction suggested by computer artists and BBS sysops, causing this exception to copyright protection to engulf the rule?"

- *Tight copyright control should be retained.* Commercial software publishers, Rose notes, are concerned about the distribution of their programs on the Net without permission. Congress recently helped by adding the threat of prison time to copyright law penalties. However, Rose concludes that "it remains to be seen whether tougher laws and industry threats will put a permanent dent in the Net's freewheeling treatment of software and other information."

Rose is correct in concluding that the Internet is out of control. Copyright infringements are so common and open that it is no longer shocking to see them occur. Part of the problem is that the Internet is an international phenomenon, and in many countries copyright laws—and attitudes about copyright in general—are much more casual than in the United States. Software manufacturers are keenly aware of the problem;

Censorship in Cyberspace

Two controversial events have triggered a torrent of criticism about censorship on the Internet and raised free-press issues in many countries.

In late 1995, CompuServe, which has a large presence in Europe, announced that it would block access to certain newsgroups that the German government found objectionable. In doing so, CompuServe soothed a German prosecutor but raised the ire of free-press advocates. What CompuServe had done, they argued, was nothing less than censorship.

Not long afterward, the U.S. Congress passed a sweeping revision of the country's telecommunications policy. In the process, it outlawed the transmission of sexually explicit and other indecent materials. The act, unfortunately, provided little guidance about what exactly constitutes explicit or indecent material. Immediately, the American Civil Liberties Union and others challenged the law's constitutionality.

Because the Internet is international in scope, it is almost impossible to enforce such a law. What one country finds objectionable may be quite suitable in another.

These actions have made it almost certain that an international treaty similar to the International Copyright Convention will have to be considered as a means of resolving such disputes. In the meantime, chaos will reign. What would happen if a German prosecutor demanded extradition of a U.S. citizen for violating German obscenity laws? Would the United States be obliged to extradite the alleged violator? There is a good chance we will find out in the years ahead.

they lose billions of dollars each year as a result of illegal copies. Much of that occurs overseas.

The fact is that software, text, sound, photos and video all are easier to duplicate in digital form than in printed or broadcast form. Further, there is no standard way of marking digitally created copies so they are identified as illegally obtained. Also, the ease with which digital copying occurs across international borders, thanks to computer networks, makes duplication almost impossible to trace and prosecution prohibitively expensive.

Journalists have a stake in the issue. Their work is copyrighted either by their employers or themselves. They have a right to expect that it will not be duplicated illegally, but it is an issue that extends far beyond the realm of journalism. As the Internet and other parts of cyberspace increasingly are used as vehicles for publishing, every such publisher will be affected. So will universities, corporations and others.

Almost certainly, this problem will not be resolved without further congressional action. An international solution will require international action and treaty revision, which often takes decades to accomplish. In the meantime, both in the United States and abroad the existing copyright laws will have to suffice. There is some protection in existing laws, to be sure, but probably not enough.

One note about a closely related topic is necessary. Some freelance journalists are furious that articles sold to newspapers and magazines have been reproduced electronically in the many online databases. They insist that constitutes republication, and as a result they should receive royalties from any additional income publishers derive from such services. Most publishers are rewriting their freelance contracts to include electronic republication rights, and freelance writers have organized to fight that action. The issue is far from settled. However, it does not affect staff writers, whose work is clearly the property of their employers.

GOVERNMENT REGULATION

In early 1996, the U.S. Congress finally got around to revising the Communications Act of 1934. The telecommunications bill it passed, and President Clinton signed, promises to revolutionize the delivery of media in the United States. The landmark legislation:

- Immediately deregulated cable television rates.
- Allowed telephone companies to deliver video to homes and businesses.
- Allowed long-distance, cable television and other companies— including public utilities such as electric companies—to offer local telephone service.
- Set aside a new chunk of airwaves for television stations to deliver digital signals.
- Awarded preferential pricing protection to schools, libraries and rural health facilities.
- Outlawed the transmission of sexually explicit and other indecent materials to minors over computer networks such as the Internet.
- Required television manufacturers to equip new sets with a computer chip that helps parents block the viewing of offensive shows by children.
- Relaxed restrictions on the ownership of television and radio stations.
- Eliminated the ban on one company from owning a television station and a cable television system in the same market.
- Generally eliminated rules that prohibit local and long-distance telephone companies and cable television franchises from entering each other's markets.

Almost simultaneously, the Federal Communications Commission announced its intention to alter its rules on cross-ownership of media outlets in a single market. Today, it is almost impossible for a company to own both a television station and a newspaper in the same city. The FCC's announcement means that such regulations are certain to be relaxed.

The impact of such sweeping deregulation is not fully clear today, but almost certainly it will speed the delivery of high-speed information delivery to the home. It also will increase the competition for that franchise and perhaps lessen the cost to consumers. In the process, it turns the media industry into a major corporate battleground. Unfortunately, while the new legislation answered many questions about the role of media in society, it left many other questions unanswered.

That is because the new telecommunications act falls far short of total deregulation of the media. Magazines and newspapers have not been regulated by government at all, and cable television will now join them in that category. However, telephone companies still will be regulated to some degree by the state and federal governments, and radio and television will continue to be regulated by the federal government. That is trouble if one believes, as most experts do, that we are headed for an era when all those media will blend into one. Who regulates that new medium? Is there any regulation at all? Isn't it good that we have some media not subject to government regulation? If all the media blend into one electronically delivered medium, isn't it likely that medium will be regulated?

Those are disturbing questions, and there are no clear-cut answers.

Radio and television are regulated by the FCC largely on the theory that the number of frequencies is limited and therefore the government must ensure free access to varying views and opinions by licensing stations and reviewing content. Newspapers and magazines are not regulated on free-press grounds and because there is no limit to the number of newspapers that can be published. Yet today's reality is that there are far more radio and television stations than newspapers, and broadcasters have free-press rights, too. Newspapers, not television, have monopolies in most U.S. cities. In short, the whole logic behind government regulation is flawed.

Congress knows that, but so far no one is quite sure how to fix it. Regulating newspapers and magazines just is not in the cards, and the idea of full deregulation of television would surely result in an outcry from those who want to monitor or eliminate sex, violence and other content.

On the state level, telephone companies remain heavily regulated. In the past, the rationale for that regulation was that telephone companies enjoyed monopolies on local service. With the passage of the new telecommunications act, that no longer will be the case. An experiment in Rochester, N.Y., to provide competition in local telephone service was the first of many nationwide. Eventually, almost all local telephone companies will be subjected to competition similar to what the long-distance companies now experience.[2]

The big question is the impact of all this on new computer-based media systems. Almost every type of media company is poised to provide new media services to the home. As magazines, newspapers, radio, television, entertainment, cable television and telephone companies— some regulated and some not—enter joint ventures to provide new media services, it is unclear how, whether or to what extent those services will be regulated.

Many believe the new media are likely to be regulated simply because the broadcast media and telephone companies, which still face some form of government regulation, will be engaged in the process. Others argue there should be no regulation because much of the content will come from newspapers, magazines and Hollywood, which are unregulated and should remain so.

Whether to regulate the new media is one question to be answered. If the answer is yes, then the next question becomes: Who does the regulation?

Congress still has some tough issues to decide as it sorts through all this. It will have to consider the world stage as well. The Internet experience shows us that no one country will decide these issues alone. Some, such as copyright, are issues for the world community.

PRIVACY AND ELECTRONIC MAIL

Another issue that has received plenty of attention in recent years is the question of whether electronic mail should be considered private (see Figure 8.1). A survey of American businesses by *MacWorld* magazine suggested that 20 million Americans may be subject to some type of electronic snooping by their bosses. More than 21 percent of respondents to the survey indicated that they have searched through others' computer files, voice mail, electronic mail or other network-based forms of communication. For large companies, the figure rises to 30 percent.[3]

Most electronic mail on corporate computer networks is archived, which means that backup tapes of those messages are available. How long such messages should be retained and who should have access to them are questions of great debate. Some companies insist that because the computers belong to the company, supervisors have every right to read what's there. Others say such communication should be protected by privacy laws.

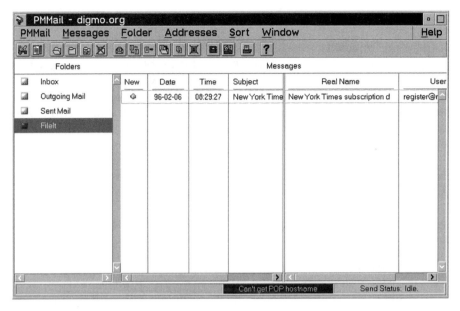

Figure 8.1   The increasing use of electronic mail creates some serious questions about privacy.

While Congress has yet to act on the issue, federal agencies are setting their own policies. For example, any defense contractor must now retain electronic mail messages for 10 years. That is to make certain that government attorneys can sort through that mail in cases in which a company is expected of cheating the government.

At what cost is such evidence protected? Should electronic mail that may help produce evidence of fraud be retained at the expense of invading someone's privacy? Should e-mail be protected just as private conversations are protected from wiretap, or should e-mail sent or received at work be treated like internal memos, retained by policy of the company?

From a journalist's perspective, can an electronic mail message from a news source be protected under the shield laws (or source-protection laws) that exist in many states, or will such communication be subject to court subpoena? Does a newspaper editor have the right to read a reporter's e-mail? Regardless of the way those issues are decided, someone is certain to be unhappy.

IMPACT ON SUNSHINE LAWS

Some of those issues also will have an impact on so-called *sunshine laws,* or open meetings laws. Now that it is possible to exchange e-mail messages instantaneously, or even have an electronic meeting on the Internet, does that constitute a meeting? What about a video teleconference? And what if those meetings take place across state lines?

Journalists will be affected by the resolution of such issues. They will have to be on the lookout for public officials who use the latest technology to circumvent the law. To ensure there is no escape clause, many laws will have to be changed. A 1994 survey showed that only two-thirds of the states now prohibit government bodies from meeting through electronic mail, online lists or computer conferences.[4]

ENDNOTES

1. "Is Copyright Dead on the Net?" by Lance Rose, *Wired*, November 1993, pp. 112–113.
2. *PC Week,* Jan. 2, 1995, p. 1.
3. *MacWorld,* July 1993, p. 120.
4. Ross, Susan Dente, "Operating in the Fog: The Uncertain Application of Sunshine Laws to Interactive Computer Technologies," academic paper presented to the Association for Education in Journalism and Mass Communication, Atlanta, Ga., August 1994.

9

THE FUTURE:
ENTER WITH CAUTION

By now, it should be obvious that the computer has forever changed the way journalism is practiced. It is also about to change the way it is delivered. Almost everyone agrees that the coming years will produce a major upheaval in the media industry as computer-based delivery systems give users access to more information on a single system with a choice of formats—text, graphics, sound and full-motion video. It is an upheaval that many fear and that many others are approaching with caution. How soon it will happen, however, is a subject of great debate.

Also subject to much debate is this: Who will be the winners and losers? The answer is that there need not be *any* losers. Let us see why.

Some believe newspapers are destined to be losers. Certainly there are signs that the newspaper industry is less than healthy. In a recent five-year period, the number of daily newspapers in the United States plunged by more than 200. While about 1,500 dailies remain, do not expect there to be that many by the turn of the century. Few cities still have competing dailies, and in cities where there is competition, only the dominant daily is profitable. The number of weeklies is declining even more rapidly. Newspapers are unlikely to disappear in the lifetime of anyone reading this book, but their influence as a news medium is clearly on the wane as more and more Americans get their news from television. Each year, the percentage of advertising that goes to newspapers decreases.[1] Finally, newspapers are an industrial product, produced each day at huge cost (paper, ink and people) and with enormous delivery problems that their electronic counterparts do not encounter. That places them at a permanent competitive disadvantage.

However, in many ways newspapers, with their large news-gathering staffs and their vast databases of local information, are ideally positioned to succeed in the new media marketplace. Their news-gathering resources are unmatched by television in almost any local market, and they understand better than any other medium how to deliver large volumes of information—both news and advertising. Those are important factors that should make newspaper companies key players in the changing media marketplace. The key for newspaper executives is to understand that they are in the business of selling information, not just newspapers.

Some believe television is ideally positioned to take advantage of the coming changes. Clearly, the broadcast industry has the technology that users crave—full-motion video, color, sound and great eye appeal. Distribution costs are extremely low compared to those of print competitors. Television has become the medium of choice; busy people, and particularly young people, simply prefer it to newspapers as a news medium. Its power as an image-building advertising medium is unquestioned.

However, television cannot deliver the large volumes of information that will be needed in the Information Age. It is saddled with antiquated analog technology in a digital era. Even the Federal Communications Commission recognizes that television's future is digital. That is why the United States rejected Japan's analog format for high-definition television in favor of digital technology. Digital information, including full-motion video, can be transmitted across cable television or telephone lines, freeing the airwaves for more cellular telephone service and similar devices. The FCC covets the bandwidth that the conversion of television to digital format will free. So television is facing a costly and wrenching transition in technology that eventually will be forced by the government if not the marketplace.

Television also must face the problem of creating an infrastructure for database services. Television reporting staffs are minuscule compared to those of newspapers in almost every U.S. city. The television industry's understanding of digital information storage and retrieval pales by comparison to that of newspapers and magazines. Their sales staffs have no experience with text-based advertising, a key ingredient of the computer-based new media of the future.

So, while both newspapers and television bring much to the table as we create the media of the future, neither has the resources and expertise to be dominant. Nor do the entertainment companies, computer companies, television companies or cable television. In the last couple of years, the brightest corporate minds in America have come to understand that.

As a result, what we have seen in recent years is a rush to form partnerships. That is why Disney bought ABC and why Westinghouse bought CBS. That is why Sears is aligned with IBM and why Microsoft has joint ventures with TCI, MCI and NBC. That is why Time Warner is investing heavily in entertainment and new media and buying Ted Turner's CNN. It is why newspapers are rushing to place their content online and diversifying rapidly. The reality is that no one company can do it all; those who will be winners are those who strike the best partnerships with others.

One thing on which all experts agree is that good content is the key to developing the media of the future. If that is true, both newspapers and television can be big winners. They have the content the public wants; for the most part, IBM, Microsoft and the Bell Operating Companies do not.

THE ROLE OF ADVERTISING

One unresolved issue surrounding the transition from the media of today to the computer-based media of the future is the question of who pays. Today, most newspaper and magazine revenue comes from advertising, and subscription costs at best cover the cost of distribution. Broadcast television's revenue comes almost exclusively from advertising, while cable television's revenue is subscription-based, and advertising plays a minor role.

The mix of revenue in new-media systems is far from clear. If services such as Prodigy and America Online are an indication, subscription revenues and advertising both will play a significant role. Almost without question, though, computer-based media will become increasingly popular with advertisers.

That is because computer-based media will have the ability to tell advertisers who read their advertisements and how long they read them. Further, computer-based media will be able to deliver exact demographic statistics. That means an advertiser will be able to determine with great precision whether advertisements are reaching the intended audience.

No existing medium can deliver that degree of assurance that advertisements are being read or watched. Nor can any existing medium provide exact demographic data. Instead, today's media rely on sampling technique to provide estimates of advertising effectiveness. Both television's Neilsen ratings and print's readership studies make assumptions about the total audience based on a small sample. However, with computer-based media, the *sample* is replaced with a *census*.

Do not forget that most of today's media, with the exception of highly specialized magazines and a few cable television channels, are mass media. They deliver to huge audiences with demographic characteristics that resemble those of the population at large. If you are selling something that everyone uses, such as soap, that is fine, but if your product is targeted for a specific audience, television and newspapers are not the best media.

The computer-based media of the future are ideal for target advertising (see Figure 9.1). The forums that will exist on almost every conceivable topic are the best places to deliver that advertising. Prodigy and America Online already are learning that. As the size of their audiences grows, advertisers will find online services even more attractive. The PIUs, an early form of computer-based media, appear to be well-positioned to cash in on the move to new media.

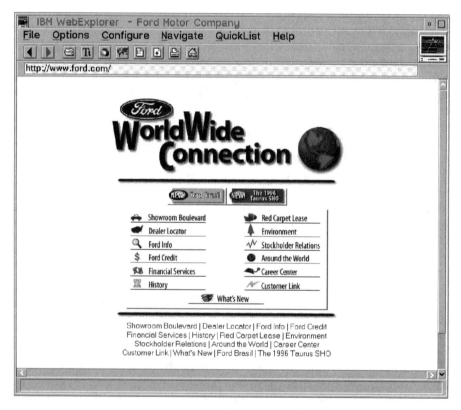

Figure 9.1 More and more advertising is appearing on the Internet, and improved ability to protect credit card transactions is expected to add to the medium's appeal.

LINKING, LAYERING AND RESEARCHING

It is important to understand that the computer-based new media are just that—an entirely new form of communication. What makes them unique is their ability to link to related sources of information, to layer information in ways that allow the consumer to accept or reject as much information as he or she chooses, and to do original research on a topic.

The linking capability is most obvious on the World Wide Web. There, good hypertext links offered by the content provider make it easy for the consumer to go to other sites for related material. No longer is the consumer limited to what the newspaper wants to write about a subject.

Layering also is attractive to users. Those who want to scan only the headlines can do so. Those who want more can go to additional layers of information on the home site or at other sites. Less sophisticated layering is present in existing media. For example, the *Wall Street Journal's* front page provides a news summary each day. Busy readers can scan that summary to get the gist of today's news; those interested in knowing more can turn to the full story inside. Layering in the new media is similar, but instead of providing two layers of information, the new media may provide hundreds of layers thanks to their ability to link to earlier stories on the same subject or to related material on computers throughout the world.

The new media also provide original research capability. The World Wide Web can now provide links to corporate or government databases previously inaccessible to news consumers. For example, a story about the growth in minority population in New York City might be linked to databases of previous years' census data. That would allow the consumer to compare current demographic statistics with the demographics of the same burrough or precinct years before. The power and potential of such capability is unlimited.

All these characteristics make the new media much more than a place to dump text, graphics, audio and video created for the existing media. As innovative pioneers help fulfill the medium's potential, the emergence of a distinct new media form will become obvious.

GATEKEEPING AND AGENDA-SETTING

From the journalist's perspective, there is one extremely troubling aspect of the transition from the news media of today to those of tomorrow: The journalist's influence is almost certain to wane.

Historically, journalists have served as gatekeepers of information, a phenomenon much studied and much discussed by communications researchers. Anyone who has ever attended a journalism or communications school knows about the Gatekeeper Theory. With the arrival of the new media, however, it is a theory that will be relegated to history.

That is because the journalist will no longer serve as a gatekeeper. All of today's media are limited in capacity by time and space. Radio and television can broadcast only so much news because of time limitations; newspapers and magazines have space limitations. Thus, until now the journalist has served as a gatekeeper, deciding which news (and other information) is allowed to pass through to consumers. It is a well-known fact that a daily newspaper publishes only a tiny fraction of the wire-service news it receives each day. Television is even more limited; its anchors in a half-hour newscast cannot even read everything on the front page of a newspaper because of time constraints.

The computer-based new media of the future will not have that limitation. They will be able to provide access to all wire-service information. Prodigy, America Online and the other PIUs, and even the Internet, already do so. Thus, the role of the journalist as gatekeeper will diminish.

Another much-discussed and much-researched phenomenon of the existing media is their role in agenda-setting. In today's society, journalists decide what is important. What the media determine to be the major stories of the day become those on which the public focuses (and the ones to which government must react).

It is interesting to speculate about how that role might diminish as we move into the new media era. With computer-delivered media, there is no necessity for a front page or a lead story. Because of that, news consumers will be able to decide for themselves what is important, and the role of the media in setting the public agenda is likely to diminish.

Some hold out hope that consumers actually *appreciate* the agenda-setting role of the media. Those who hold that view believe it is reasonable to assume that consumers will *want* or even *demand* a journalist-prepared list of the day's top stories. More likely, some will appreciate the help and others will prefer to do it themselves. Do not forget that computers will be able to help consumers sort through the massive amount of information available. It will be possible with computer-based media systems for each user to program the computer to retrieve articles, sound clips or video clips about topics of interest.

What all this means is that journalists are facing a major change in their role in society. As we approach the future, journalists will not be able to afford the luxury of obstinance they have enjoyed in the past. No longer will haughty journalists be able to say, "I know what is best for my readers (or viewers), and that is what I am going to give them." For journalists to succeed in the new-media world of the future, they will have to understand marketing. They will be forced to deliver what the user wants.

To be heard in the future, journalists also will have to produce good material worth consuming. The schlock too often delivered in the past will not cut it. It will be an increasingly competitive world for the consumer's attention. Only by delivering high-quality journalism will the media be able to maintain some degree of influence in agenda-setting.

A FINAL NOTE

If the years ahead appear to be difficult ones for the media, they also will be exciting ones. We stand on the threshold of a huge transformation in the way our society receives and consumes information. Journalism jobs that now exist will disappear; others will be created that do not now exist. Although ways of consuming information will change, the thirst for information will only increase. Journalists are the people who provide that information, and they will continue to be in great demand.

ENDNOTE

1. Facts about Newspapers, an annual publication of the Newspaper Association of America, Reston, Va.

Appendix A

ANNOTATED BIBLIOGRAPHY

CompuServe Magazine, P.O. Box 20212, Columbus, Ohio 43220. A magazine published by CompuServe that is useful in finding your way through its maze of services.

Digital Media, P.O. Box 644, Media, Pa. 19063. A wonderful but expensive ($395 a year) newsletter for keeping abreast of the latest developments in new media technology, particularly industry alliances and technological advances.

Dizard, Wilson. *Old Media, New Media: Mass Communications in the Information Age,* Longman, White Plains, N.Y., 1994. An overview of the changing media landscape but with little practical value for the newcomer to the online world.

Estrada, Susan. *Connecting to the Internet,* O'Reilly & Associates, Sebastopol, Calif., 1993. Contains practical advice on connecting to the Internet.

Glossbrenner, Alfred. *How to Look It Up Online: Get the Information Edge with Your Personal Computer,* St. Martin's Press, New York, 1987. Comprehensive, if somewhat dated, guide to online research.

Internet World, 20 Ketchum St., Westport, Conn. 06880. An excellent source of current information about the Internet.

Koch, Tom. *Journalism for the 21st Century: Online Information, Electronic Databases and the News,* Praeger Publishers, New York, 1991. An academic approach to the subject that is useful but somewhat ponderous.

Krol, Ed. *The Whole Internet User's Guide and Catalog,* O'Reilly & Associates, Sebastopol, Calif., 1994. A thorough guide to Internet resources.

Lui, Cricket; Peek, Jerry; Jones, Russ; Buus, Bryan; and Nye, Adrian. *Managing Internet Information Services,* O'Reilly & Associates, Sebastopol, Calif., 1994. An excellent guide for those planning to start and manage Internet sites.

NetGuide, 600 Community Drive, Manhasset, N.Y. 11030. A magazine devoted to the Internet and the PIUs.

New Media, P.O. Box 1771, Riverton, N.J. 08077-7371. A monthly magazine that keeps abreast of new media developments. Particularly good for its coverage of CD-ROMs.

Online Access, 5615 W. Cermak Road, Cicero, Ill. 60650-2290. A magazine devoted to the online community published 10 times a year. Includes excellent coverage of Internet issues, bulletin boards and the PIUs.

Paul, Nora. *Computer-Assisted Research: A Guide to Tapping Online Information,* 2nd ed., The Poynter Institute, St. Petersburg, Fla., 1994. An excellent summary of online resources prepared by a trained journalism librarian. Brief and to the point.

Pavlik, John V. *New Media Technology: Cultural and Commercial Perspectives,* Allyn & Bacon, Needham Heights, Mass., 1996. An excellent perspective on the development of new media and their impact on society.

Weinberg, Steve. *The Reporter's Handbook: An Investigator's Guide to Documents and Techniques,* 3rd ed., St. Martin's Press, New York, 1996. The definitive handbook for investigative reporters.

Wired, P.O. Box 191826, San Francisco, Calif. 94119–9866. A whacky, offbeat and extremely useful source of information about cyberspace in magazine format.

Appendix B

GLOSSARY

Analog A transmission scheme used in telephonic communications. Analog data must be translated into digital form before they can be processed in a computer.

Archie A search program for locating files stored on FTP servers.

Asynchronous communication A transmission method in which start and stop bits are used to define each character.

Bandwidth The amount of data that can be carried on a given circuit.

Baud rate The speed of transmission used by modems.

Bit One-eighth of a byte.

Boolean connectors Terms used as delimiters in searching computerized databases.

Browser A computer program with a graphical user interface that makes it easy for someone to navigate the Internet's World Wide Web.

Bulletin board In computer context, a host computer on which an operator allows those with similar interests to send and receive messages and transfer computer programs.

Byte A term used to describe a collection of eight computerized bits of information that produce a character.

Cable modem A device used to allow the transmission of digital data over standard cable television lines.

Carrier signal A sound output by a modem that allows it to connect to another modem. A carrier signal must be established before computer data can be transferred.

CD-ROMs Compact disks that in many cases contain information of use to journalists in easily accessible form. Also commonly used for audio recordings and games.

Commercial databases   Computerized repositories of articles previously published in newspapers or magazines or broadcast by radio and television stations.

Cyberspace   A term used to describe the entire world of online services.

Digital   Signals used to transfer information within and among computers.

DNS   Domain Name System. A structure for translating numeric Internet addresses into strings of words denoting user names and locations.

Fiber optics   A high-speed method of transferring digital data over glass optical fibers. Expensive to install.

Finger   Software used to determine whether another user is logged onto the Internet.

FTP   File Transfer Protocol. This protocol makes it possible to transfer files between a host computer and a remote one. It is used often to upload (transmit) or download (receive) software.

Gopher   A search tool developed at the University of Minnesota (whose mascot is the Golden Gopher). Before Mosaic and the WWW, Gopher was the best way to navigate the Internet, and it is still widely used. Gopher sites are accessible through most WWW browsers.

GUI   Graphical User Interface. An enhanced way of navigating the Internet using text and graphics.

HTML   HyperText Markup Language. The language used to design World Wide Web pages for the Internet.

Hypertext   A link within a document or page that links the user to related material simply by clicking on the link with a mouse.

Internet   A worldwide computer network originally started by government but privatized in the 1990s.

IRC   Internet Relay Chat. Software that allows keyboarded live discussions across the Internet.

ISDN   Integrated Services Digital Network. A high-speed means of digital communication over telephone lines.

Listserv   List Server. A listserv is a mailing list feature that enables users interested in a specific topic to send a message to all subscribers to the list without individual addressing. In most cases, you can subscribe to a listserv by sending an e-mail message to its address. In the body of the message, type *subscribe* (or *sub*) *carr-l [your name]*.

Local area network (LAN)   A means of linking computers within a given area.

Modem   A device that translates analog signals to digital form and vice versa. Short for modulator-demodulator.

Morgue The computerized library of a newspaper, magazine or broadcast station.

Mosaic A computer program developed at the University of Illinois that made the World Wide Web popular. A browser.

Netscape The most popular of the World Wide Web browsers.

Newsgroup A forum or conference area where you can post public messages and exchange ideas with others interested in a specific topic. There are thousands of such forums on Usenet, part of the Internet. Newsgroups can be of immense value to journalists searching for experts on a topic. Simply post a message and wait for the replies to roll in.

PING A TCP/IP utility that sends packets of information on the network. It is used to determine whether a computer is connected to the Internet.

PPP Point-to-Point Protocol. One of the two major protocols used by Internet service providers to connect users to the Internet by telephone.

Public information utilities (PIUs) Commercial databases that cater to consumers, including CompuServe, America Online, Prodigy and the MSNBC.

Serial port A device built into a computer that permits the attachment of modems and other serial devices. Computers also often have parallel ports.

SLIP Serial Line Interface Protocol. One of the two major protocols used by Internet service providers to connect users to the Internet by telephone.

SMTP Simple Mail Transfer Protocol. A protocol that allows electronic mail to move from point to point on the Internet.

Synchronous communication A transmission method in which a group of characters or block of data is sent as a continuous stream of bits.

TCP/IP Transmission Control Protocol/Internet Protocol. The standard for communication on the Internet.

Telnet A terminal emulation protocol that permits a user to log on to another computer on the Internet.

URL Uniform Resource Locator. An Internet address used by the World Wide Web. It begins with http (short for *hypertext transfer protocol*).

Usenet User Network. A public network made up of thousands of discussion groups, called newsgroups. Newsgroups are organized by topic.

Veronica Another search tool similar to Archie. It searches text that appears in Gopher menus.

Voice-grade lines The lowest level of telephone circuit. Better circuits are conditioned for high-level voice or digital data.

WAIS   Wide Area Information Server. WAIS is software that indexes large text files in computer databases. Users use keywords to help locate material of interest.

Winsock   Windows Socket. An application programming interface (API) designed to allow Windows applications like Mosaic to run over a TCP/IP network.

World Wide Web   The most popular part of the Internet. It allows users to navigate the Internet with ease using graphical user interfaces.

Appendix C

INTERNET ADDRESSES OF NEWS PROVIDERS

This list of media computer addresses was compiled by searching through various resources on the Internet. By nature, the Internet is a changing environment. Sites come and go almost daily. Therefore, this list should be used as a starting point for exploring the Internet. It is not intended as a comprehensive source of Internet media resources.

DAILY NEWSPAPERS

Abilene, Texas: *Abilene Reporter-News*
http://www.abilene.com/arn/arnhome.html

Akron, Ohio: *Beacon Journal* (sports)
http://www.beaconjournal.com

Anderson, Ind.: *Herald-Bulletin*
http://www.indol.com/io_mmenu.html

Anderson, S.C.: *Anderson Independent-Mail*
http://www.globalvision.net/ANDERSON/index.html

Annapolis, Md.: *The Capital* (calendar)
http://www.infi.net/capital

Asbury Park, N.J.: *Asbury Park Press*
http://www.injersey.com/Media/PressNet/

Atlanta: *Atlanta Journal-Constitution*
http://www.ajc.com/home.htm

Atlantic City, N.J.: *The Press*
  http://www.acy.digex.net/~acpress/acpress.html

Austin, Texas: *Austin American-Statesman* (sports)
  http://hookem.com

Bakersfield, Calif.: *Bakersfield Californian*
  http://www.kern.com/tbc/

Beaver, Pa.: *Beaver County Times*
  http://www.pgh.net/beaver/about.html

Bedford, Ind.: *Times-Mail*
  http://www.intersource.com/~tmnews

Beloit, Wis.: *Beloit Daily News*
  http://www.bossnt.com/bdn.html

Bentonville, Ark.: *Benton County Daily Record*
  http://nwanews.com

Birmingham, Ala.: *Birmingham Post-Herald*
  http://www.the-matrix.com/ph/ph.html

Bloomington, Ind.: *The Herald-Times* (magazine)
  http://www.intersource.com/~bcmag/

Boston: *The Boston Globe*
  http://www.globe.com

Carlisle, Pa.: *The Sentinel*
  http://www1.trib.com/CUMBERLINK/

Casper, Wyo.: *Star-Tribune*
  http://www.trib.com

Cedar Rapids, Iowa: *The Gazette*
  http://www.infi.net/fyiowa/gazette

Charleston, S.C.: *The Post and Courier*
  http://www.charleston.net

Chattanooga, Tenn.: *The Free Press*
  http://www.chatfreepress.com/index.html

Chattanooga, Tenn.: *The Times*
  http://www.chattimes.com/index.html

Chicago: *Chicago Sun-Times*
  http://www.suntimes.com

Chicago: *Chicago Tribune* (employment advertisements)
  http://www.chicago.tribune.com/

Chicago: *Chicago Tribune* (technology news)
  http://www.chicago.tribune.com/coffee/

Christian Science Monitor
  http://freerange.com/csmonitor

Clarksburg, W.Va.: *Clarksburg Exponent-Telegram*
http://cpubco.com

Colorado Springs, Colo.: *Gazette Telegraph*
http://usa.net/cgi-bin/gazette

Columbia, Mo.: *The Daily Tribune*
http://www.trib.net/

Columbia, Mo.: *The Missourian*
http://digmo.org/

Columbia, S.C.: *The State*
http://www.infi.net/thestate

Columbus, Ohio: *Columbus Dispatch*
http://www.cd.columbus.oh.us

Columbus, Ohio: *Daily Reporter*
http://www.sddt.com/~columbus/

Computer News Daily
http://nytsyn.com/cgi-bin/times/lead/go

Concord, N.H.: *Concord Monitor*
http://www.cmonitor.com/

Corpus Christi, Texas: *Caller-Times*
http://wwwtrn.luk.net/cchome/

Dallas: *Dallas Morning News* (editorials)
http://www.pic.net/tdmn/

Danbury, Conn.: *Danbury News-Times*
http://www.danbury.lib.ct.us/media/news/

Dayton, Ohio: *Dayton Daily News*
http://www.access-dayton.com

Denver: *Denver Post Empire* (magazine)
http://www.denverpost.com/empire

Detroit: *Detroit Free Press*
gopher://gopher.det-freepress.com:9002

Detroit: *Detroit News*
http://detnews.com

Dover and Laconia, N.H.: *Fosters Daily Democrat* and *The Citizen*
http://www.fosters.com/

East Brunswick, N.J.: *Home News and Tribune*
http://www.injersey.com/Media/HNT/

Elyria, Ohio: *The Chronicle-Telegram*
http://www.ohio.net/~mathlida/ect.html

Evansville, Ind.: *The Evansville Courier*
http://www.evansville.net/newsweb/

Fayetteville, N.C.: *Observer-Times*
http://www.infi.net/FOTO/

Framingham, Mass.: *Middlesex News*
gopher://ftp.std.com/11/periodicals/Middlesex-News

Ft. Lauderdale, Fla.: *Sun-Sentinel* (entertainment)
http://www.xso.com/index.htm

Gainesville, Fla.: *Gainesville Sun*
http://www.jou.ufl.edu/enews/sun

Galveston, Texas: *Galveston County Daily News*
http://www.galvnews.com/

Glen Falls, N.Y.: *Post-Star*
http://www.albany.globalone.net/poststar/

Greensboro, N.C.: *News & Record*
http://www.infi.net/nr/triad.html

Hackensack, N.J.: *The Bergen Record*
http://www.bergen.com

Hanover, Pa.: *Hanover Evening Sun*
http://www.sun-link.com

Hartford, Conn.: *Hartford Courant*
http://www.atlantic.com/ctguide/news/courant/

Hastings, Neb.: *Hastings Tribune*
http://www.cnweb.com/tribune

Houston: *Houston Chronicle*
http://www.chron.com/

Huntsville, Ala.: *Huntsville Times*
http://www.traveller.com/htimes

Indianapolis, Ind.: *Indianapolis Star and News*
http://www.starnews.com

Jacksonville, N.C.: *Daily News*
http://www.eastnc.coastalnet.com/cnmedia/jdnews/breaker1.htm

Journal Link (*Wall Street Journal* advertisements)
http://www.adnet.wsj.com

Kailua-Kona, Hawaii: *West Hawaii Today*
http://www.ilhawaii.net/~wht

Keene, N.H.: *Keene Sentinel*
http://www.keenesentinel.com

Knoxville, Tenn.: *The Knoxville News-Sentinel*
http://www.knoxnews.com

Kokomo, Ind.: *Kokomo Herald*
http://www.holli.com/herald/

Lafayette, Ind.: *Journal and Courier*
http://matrix.mdn.com:/jconline/

Lawrence, Kan.: *Lawrence Journal-World*
http://www.ljworld.com

Lebanon, Mo.: *Daily Record*
http://www.llion.org/ldr/news.html

Lehighton, Pa.: *Times News*
http://www.tnonline.com/sports.net/

Lewiston, Idaho: *Lewiston Morning Tribune*
http://www.lmtribune.com

Lexington, Ky.: *Lexington Herald-Leader*
http://www.kentuckyconnect.com/heraldleader/

Lincoln, Neb.: *Lincoln Journal Star*
http://newsone.com/

Little Rock, Ark.: *Arkansas Democrat-Gazette*
http://www.ardemgaz.com

Louisville, Ky.: *Courier-Journal*
http://iglou.com/gizweb

Madison, Wis.: *Capital Times* and *State Journal*
http://www.madison.com

Mankato, Minn.: *Mankato Free Press*
http://www.ic.mankato.mn.us/news/news/freepress.html

Marietta, Ohio: *Marietta Times*
gopher://seorf.ohiou.edu:2001/11/seorf.stuff/Med

Maui, Hawaii: *Maui News*
http://www.maui.net/~mauinews/news.html

Medina, Ohio: *Medina County Gazette*
http://www.ohio.net/gazette/

Milwaukee: *Milwaukee Journal-Sentinel* (professional football)
http://www.packerplus.com/

Minneapolis-St. Paul: *Pioneer-Press*
http://www.pioneerplanet.com

Minneapolis-St. Paul: *Star Tribune*
http://www.startribune.com/

Missoula, Mont.: *Missoulian*
http://www.missoulian.com

Mobile, Ala.: *Mobile Press Register*
http://www.mobol.com

Munster, Ind.: *Calunet Times*
http://www.calunet.com

Myrtle Beach, S.C.: *Myrtle Beach Herald*
http://city-info.com/mbh/main.html

Newark, N.J.: *Newark Star-Ledger* (weather)
http://www.nj.com

New Bedford, Mass.: *The Standard-Times*
http://www.s-t.com/newstandard

New York: *Investor's Business Daily*
http://ibd.ensemble.com/tryit.html

New York: *Newsday*
http://www.newsday.com/

New York: *New York Times* (fax using Acrobat)
http://nytimesfax.com

New York Times
http://www.nytimes.com

New York: *Your Daily Health*
http://nytsyn.com/medic/

Norfolk, Va.: *The Virginian-Pilot*
http://www.infi.net/pilot/

Philadelphia: *Inquirer and Daily News*
http://www.phillynews.com

Phoenix: *Arizona Republic and Phoenix Gazette*
http://www.azcentral.com

Pittsburgh: *Pittsburgh Tribune-Review*
http://tribune-review.com/trib/

Portland, Maine: *Portland Press Herald*
http://www.portland.net/ph/

Pottsville, Pa.: *Pottsville Republican*
http://pottsville.com

Quincy, Ill.: *The Quincy Herald-Whig*
http://www.bcl.net/~whig

Raleigh, N.C.: *The News and Observer*
http://www.nando.net

Roanoke, Va.: *Roanoke Times*
http://www.infi.net/roatimes

Rochester, N.Y.: *Democrat* and *Chronicle-Times-Union* (sports)
http://www.RochesterDandC.com/index.html

Roseburg, Ore.: *The News-Review*
http://www.oregonnews.com

Salisbury, Md.: *The Daily Times*
http://shore.intercom.net/dailytimes/

Salt Lake City: *Deseret News*
   http://www.desnews.com

Salt Lake City: *Salt Lake Tribune*
   http://www.sltrib.com

San Angelo, Texas: *Standard-Times*
   http://www.texaswest.com/

San Diego: *Transcript*
   http://www.uniontrib.com

San Diego: *Union-Tribune*
   http://www.sddt.com/

San Francisco: *Chronicle*
   http://www.sfgate.com/chronicle/index.shtml

San Francisco: *Examiner*
   http://www.sfgate.com/examiner/index.html

San Jose, Calif.: *San Jose Mercury News*
   http://www.sjmercury.com/

San Mateo, Calif.: *San Mateo Times*
   http://www.baynet.com/smtimes.html

Santa Ana, Calif.: *Orange County Register*
   http://www.ocregister.com/

Santa Rosa, Calif.: *The Press Democrat*
   http://www.pressdemo.com/library

Seattle: *Daily Journal of Commerce*
   http://www.djc.com/

Sioux City, Iowa: *Sioux City Journal*
   http://www1.trib.com/scjournal/

South Bend, Ind.: *South Bend Tribune*
   http://www.sbtinfo.com/

Spartanburg, S.C.: *Herald-Journal*
   http://www.teleplex.net/SHJ/smith/

St. Louis: *St. Louis Post-Dispatch*
   http://web1.stlnet.com/postnet/

St. Petersburg, Fla.: *St. Petersburg Times*
   http://www.sptimes.com

Syracuse, N.Y.: *Syracuse Newspapers*
   http://www.syracuse.com

Tacoma, Wash.: *The News Tribune*
   http://www.tribnet.com/

Telluride, Colo.: *Telluride Daily Planet*
   http://www.telluridegateway.com

Troy, N.Y.: *The Record*
http://www.albany.globalone.net/RECORD/

Tucson, Ariz.: *Arizona Daily Star*
http://azstarnet.com

USA Today
http://www.usatoday.com

Vacaville, Calif.: *Vacaville Reporter*
http://www.thereporter.com/

Vail, Colo.: *Vail Daily News*
http://www.realinfo.com/clients/vail

Wall Street Journal Money and Investing Update
http://update.wsj.com

Wall Street Journal Personal Edition
http://www.dowjones.com/pj.html

Washington, D.C., suburbs: *Journal* and *Express*
http://www.infi.net/journal

Washington, D.C.: *Washington Times*
http://www.washtimes-weekly.com/

Wichita Falls, Texas: *Times Record News*
http://www.wtr.com

Wilmington, N.C.: *The Morning Star*
http://www.wilmington.net/starnews/

Winona, Minn.: *Winona Daily News*
http://www.luminet.net/winnet

NONDAILY NEWSPAPERS

Anchorage, Alaska: *Alaska Journal of Commerce*
http://www.alaska.net/~journal

Aspen, Colo.: *Aspen Times*
http://www.aspenonline.com/clients/aspenonline/directory/times/
timesindex.html

Athens, Ohio: *Athens Messenger and News*
gopher://seorf.ohiou.edu:2001/11/seorf.stuff/Med

Atlanta: *Creative Loafing*
http://www.cln.com

Atmore, Ala.: *Atmore Voice*
http://www.atmore.gulf.net/~atmvoice

Austin, Texas: *Austin Chronicle*
http://www.auschron.com

Avalon, Calif.: *Catalina Islander*
http://www.catalina.com/islander/

Baltimore: *City Paper*
http://www.citypaper.com/

Baltimore: *The Afro-American*
http://199.186.169.35/

Bloomfield, Iowa: *The Bloomfield Democrat*
http://www.netins.net/showcase/bdemo/

Boston: *Bay Windows*
http://www.baywindows.com/pridenet/bw

Boston: *Business Journal*
http://citymedia.com/bbj/

Boston: *Phoenix*
http://www.phx.com/

Boulder, Colo.: *Boulder County Business Report*
http://bcn.boulder.co.us/business/BCBR/center.html

Burlington, Vt.: *Greater Burlington Business Digest*
http://together.net/~mo_busy/

Cape May, N.J.: *Star and Wave*
http://www.acy.digex.net/~cmwave/

Charleston, S.C.: *Upwith Herald*
http://www.sc.net/organizations/upwith-herald/upwith-herald.html

Charlottesville, Va.: *Real Estate Weekly*
http://www.whitlock.com/weekly

Chicago suburbs: *Pioneer Press* (47 community newspapers)
http://www.pioneerlocal.com/

Cleveland: *Crain's Cleveland Business*
http://www.crainscleveland.com

Columbia, S.C.: *The Point*
http://www.cris.com/~Scpoint/

Columbus, Ohio: *Columbus Alive*
http://www.columbuspages.com/Alive/

Dallas: *The Met*
http://themet.computek.net/

Delta, Colo.: *Delta County Independent*
http://www.dci-press.com

Detroit: *Crain's Detroit Business*
http://bizserve.com

Durango, Colo.: *Four Corners Business Journal*
http://www.4corners.com/fcbj/fcbj.html

Fairfield County, Conn.: *Acorn Press* (several newspapers)
http://www.webcom.com/acorn/

Galesburg, Ill.: *Zephyr*
http://www.misslink.net/zephyr/frontpg.htm

Grass Valley, Calif.: *The Union*
http://www.TheUnion.com/TheUnion.html

Gurdon, Ark.: *The Gurdon Times*
http://wolfden.swsc.k12.ar.us/times/

Half Moon Bay, Calif.: *Half Moon Bay Review*
http://www.hmbreview.com/hmbreview/hmbreview.html

Hartford, Conn.: *Hartford Advocate*
http://www.advocateweekly.com/

Hatch, N.M.: *Courier*
http://www.zianet.com/files/users/wblase/courier

Heber City, Utah: *The Wasatch Wave*
http://www.ditell.com/~tomnoff/

High Point, N.C.: *Archdale-Trinity News*
http://www2.hpe.com/atn/index.html

High Point, N.C.: *ESP*
http://www2.interpath.net:80/hpe/esp/

High Point, N.C.: *Triad Business News*
http://www.hpe.com/hpe/tbn/

Hollis-Brookline, N.H.: *Hollis Brookline Journal*
http://www.jlc.net/HBJ/Home.html

Hollywood, Calif.: *Baseline (Variety, Hollywood Reporter, Cable World and Village Voice)*
http://www.pkbaseline.com

Houston: *Public News*
http://www.neosoft.com/publicnews

Houston: *Texas Triangle*
http://www.outline.com/triangle/hp.html

Huntsville, Ala.: *Huntsville Extra*
http://iquest.com/~extra/nuvo

Indianapolis: *Nuvo Newsweekly*
http://www.inetdirect.net/hammer/colindex.html

Inglewood, Calif.: *Pakistan Link*
http://www.kaiwan.com/~pakistan

Iowa City, Iowa: *Icon*
http://www.jeonet.com/icon/

Jackson, Miss.: *Mississippi Business Journal*
http://www.inst.com/mbj/

Kansas City, Mo.: *Pitch Weekly*
http://www.qni.com/pitch/

Kokomo, Ind.: *Kokomo Herald*
http://www.holli.com/herald

Lafayette, Colo.: *Lafayette News*
http://www.adone.com/lafayett/index.htm

Lake Tahoe, Nev.: *Lake Tahoe News Network*
http://www.sierra.net/tahoe.com/

Lewisboro, N.Y.: *The Lewisboro Ledger*
http://www.webcom.com/acorn/lewis.html

Libby, Mont.: *The Western News*
http://www.libby.org/WesternNews/Welcome.html

Livonia and Redford, Mich.: *Observer* and *Eccentric*
http://oeonline.com

Long Island, N.Y.: *Yankee Trader*
http://www.yankeetrader.com

Los Altos, Calif.: *Los Altos Town Crier*
http://www.baynet.com/latc/

Los Angeles: *Kohtakt Russian*
http://www.pacificnet.net/~infopress

Los Angeles: *LA Weekly*
http://mosaic.echonyc.com/~voice/laweekly.htm

Louisville, Colo.: *Louisville Times*
http://www.adone.com/louisvle/index.htm

Madison, Wis.: *Isthmus*
http://www.thedailypage.com

Malden, Mass.: *Malden Milestone*
http://www.milestones.com/civitas/ma/malden/malden.html

Mammoth Lakes, Calif.: *Mammoth Times*
http://mammothtimes.com/

Marin County, Calif.: *The Slant*
http://www.rahul.net/tyler/slant.html

Maui, Hawaii: *Haleakala Times*
http://www.maui.net/~haltimes/home.html

Maui, Hawaii: *Lahaina News*
http://www.maui.net/~daveray/lahaina.html

Milford, N.H.: *Milford Cabinet*
http://www.jlc.net/Cabinet/Home.html

Milwaukee: *Business Journal*
http://citymedia.com/mbj

Milwaukee: *Shepherd-Express*
http://www.shepherd-express.com/

Minneapolis: *City Pages*
http://www.citypages.com

Minneapolis/St. Paul: *CityBusiness*
http://www.citybusiness.com/cbhome/cbhome.html

Montara, Calif.: *Montara ePress*
http://www.hax.com/Montara/MontaraMountain.html

Nantucket, Mass.: *The Inquirer and Mirror*
http://www.Nantucket.net/Inky M/

Nashville: *Nashville Business Journal*
http://www.infi.net/nc5/nbj/

Nashville: *Nashville Scene*
http://www.nashscene.com/

New Orleans: *New Orleans CityBusiness*
http://www.nopg.com

Newtown, Conn.: *The Newtown Bee*
http://www.connix.com:80/thebee/bweb/thebee.htm

New York: *AdOne/New York Press*
http://www.adone.com/

New York: *Earth Times*
http://www.igc.apc.org/earthtimes/

New York: *Jewish Post*
http://www.jewishpost.com/jewishpost/

New York: *News India-Times*
http://www2.ios.com/~newsindi/

New York: *The Network Journal*
http://www.tnj.com

New York: *The Village Voice*
http://www.villagevoice.com/

New York: *Yankee Trader*
http://www.yankeetrader.com

Oakland, Calif.: *Classified Flea Market*
http://www.cfm.com/cfm

Occidental, Calif.: *Albion Monitor*
http://www.monitor.net/monitor

Ocean City, Md.: *Times-Press*
http://www.intercom.net/biz/atbeach/news.html

Pacifica, Calif.: *Pacifica Tribune*
http://www.ci.pacifica.ca.us/TRIBUNE/

Palo Alto, Calif.: *Palo Alto Weekly*
http://www.service.com/PAW/home.html

Paonia, Colo.: *High Country News*
http://www.infosphere.com/clients/HCNArchive

Philadelphia: *Philadelphia City Paper*
http://www.cpcn.com/

Pittsburgh: *In Pittsburgh*
http://www.inpgh.com/

Pittston, Pa.: *The Pittston Gazette*
http://www.microserve.net/microserve/pitgaz/index.html

Portland, Maine: *Casco Bay Weekly*
http://www.maine.com/cbw

Portland, Maine: *Coastal Beacon*
http://www.mbeacon.com/beacon.html

Portland, Ore.: *Northwest Neighbor*
http://www.teleport.com/~neighbor/

Portland, Ore.: *Rental Property Reporter*
http://www.annco.com/reporter/rpr.htm

Port Townsend, Wash.: *Leader*
http://www.olympus.net/biz/leader/leader.html

Prescott, Ark.: *Nevada County Picayune*
http://wolfden.swsc.k12.ar.us/picayune/

Providence, R.I.: *Providence Business News*
http://www.pbn.com

Redmond, Wash.: *Northwest News*
http://www.medio.net/nwnews/

Rochester, N.Y.: *Business Strategies*
http://www.bizstrat.com

Rochester, N.Y.: *Rochester Business Journal*
http://www.rbj.net

Roundtop, Texas: *Roundtop Register*
http://rtis.com/reg/roundtop

Saco, Maine: *Southern Maine Coastal Beacon*
http://www.mbeacon.com/beacon

San Antonio: *La Prensa*
http://www.hispanic.com/LaPrensa/LaPrensa.html

San Diego: *East County Online*
http://www.sandiego-online.com/eco/main.html

San Francisco: *Bay Area BusinessWomen's Calendar*
http://www.slip.net/~bizwomen

San Francisco: *Beacon*
http://www.well.com/user/beacon

San Francisco: *Cyberspace Today*
http://www.cybertoday.com/cybertoday/

San Francisco: *Jewish Bulletin of Northern California*
http://www.jewish.com/jb

San Francisco: *San Francisco Bay Guardian*
http://www.sfbayguardian.com

San Jose, Calif.: *Metro* (multiple)
http://www.boulevards.com/metroactive

San Jose, Calif.: *OutNOW!*
http://www.zoom.com/outnow/

San Jose, Calif.: *Times* (multiple)
http://www.ipac.net/tng/tnghome.html

Seattle: *Real Change*
http://www.speakeasy.org

Seattle: *Washington Free Press*
http://www.cyberspace.com/~mrobesch/wfp.html

Sisters, Ore.: *The Nugget*
http://www.nuggetnews.com/

Spokane, Wash.: *Exchange Nickel Want Ads*
http://www.iea.com/~adlinkex

St. Paul, Minn.: *The Riverview Times*
http://oldmanriver.com/oldmanriver/

Sun Valley, Idaho: *Idaho Mountain Express*
http://www.mtexpress.com/

Sun Valley, Idaho: *The Wood River Journal*
http://www.sunvalleyid.com/wrj/

Syracuse, N.Y.: *The Syracuse New Times*
http://www.rway.com/newtimes/

Tallahassee, Fla.: *Tallahassee News*
http://www.polaris.net/~mikems

Tampa, Fla.: *Hyde Park Metro*
http://www.hpmetro.com/

Tampa, Fla.: *The Review*
http://www.review.net

Telluride, Colo.: *Telluride Times-Journal*
http://www.adone.com/ttj/index.htm

Traverse City, Mich.: *Grand Traverse Business News*
http://www.traverse.com/a&m/biznews.html

Tucson, Ariz.: *Tucson Weekly*
http://desert.net/tw/twhome.htm

Vail, Colo.: *The Vail Trail*
http://vail.net/vail_trail.html

Wasatch, Utah: *Wasatch Wave*
http://ditell.com:80/~tomnoff/

Wellington/Royal Palm Beach, Fla.: *Town-Crier*
http://www.adone.com/crier/index.htm

West Dover, Vt.: *Deerfield Valley News*
http://www.sover.net/~dvalnews/

CAMPUS NEWSPAPERS

American University: *The Eagle*
http://www.eagle.american.edu

Andrews University: *Student Movement*
http://www.andrews.edu/~smeditor

Arizona: *Arizona Daily Wildcat*
http://www.arizona.edu/pubs/wildcat/wildcat.html

Arizona State: *The State Press*
http://aspin.asu.edu/provider/StatePress/

Binghampton: *Pipe Dream*
http://www.vive.com/connect/pipedream/

Biola: *The Chimes*
http://www.biola.edu/orgs/chimes/

Bradley: *Bradley Scout*
http://www.bradley.edu/campusorg/scout/

Brigham Young: *The Daily Universe*
http://newsline.byu.edu

Brown: *The Brown Daily Herald*
http://www.netspace.org/herald/

Bucknell: *The Bucknellian*
   http://www.bucknell.edu/bucknellian
Buffalo State College: *The Record*
   http://www.snybuf.edu/~bengal/bengal.htm
Butler: *Collegian*
   http://www.butler.edu/www/collegian/collegian.html
Cal State—Chico: *The Orion*
   http://orion.csuchico.edu
Cal State—Fullerton: *Daily Titan*
   http://www5.fullerton.edu/titan/hometitan.html
Cal State—Long Beach: *Daily Forty-Niner*
   http://www.csulb.edu/~d49er/index.html
Cal State—Long Beach: *The Long Beach Union*
   http://www.csulb.edu/~union/index.html
Cal—Berkeley: *Daily Cal*
   http://server.Berkeley.EDU/DailyCal/
Cal—San Diego: *Guardian*
   http://www.ucsd.edu/guardian
Cal—Santa Barbara: *The Daily Nexus*
   http://www.mcl.ucsb.edu/nexus/
Case Western: *The Observer*
   http://www.cwru.edu/1/campus.info/observer/
Central Florida: *InPrint*
   http://www.digimark.net:80/inprint
Central Piedmont Community College: *The Spark*
   http://cpcc.cc.nc.us/pubs/studpub/studpub.htm
Chicago, University of: *Chicago Maroon*
   http://student-www.uchicago.edu/orgs/maroon/
Cincinnati: *The News Record*
   http://www.uc.edu/www/newsrecord/
Clark: *The Scarlet*
   http://aleph0.clarku.edu/~mfourche/scarlethome.html
Colby College: *The Colby Echo*
   http://colby.edu
Colgate: *The Colgate Maroon-News*
   http://149.43.10.170/maroon/
Colorado: *Campus Press*
   http://bcn.boulder.co.us/campuspress/Presshome.html

Colorado—Denver: *CU Denver Advocate*
http://www.cudenver.edu/public/advocate/index.html

Columbia: *Modern Times*
http://www.columbia.edu/cu/mt/mt.html

Columbia: *Slant*
http://pulitzer.jrn.columbia.edu/~rst10/

Columbia: *The Columbia Spectator*
http://www.columbia.edu/cu/spectator/

Cornell: *Cornell Political Forum*
http://cpf.slife.cornell.edu/

Dakota State: *The Eastern*
http://www.dsu.edu/eastern/eastern.html

Dartmouth: *The Dartmouth*
http://www.dartmouth.edu/pages/thed

Dartmouth: *The Sports Weekly*
http://www.dartmouth.edu/pages/org/tsw/weekly.html

Duke: *The Chronicle*
http://woodward.chronicle.duke.edu

Duquesne: *Duquesne Duke*
http://dig-duke.duq-duke.duq.edu

Eastern Illinois: *Daily Eastern News*
http://www.eiu.edu/today.html

Eastern Washington: *The Easterner*
http://ewu67447.ewu.edu/Easterner/EASTERNR.HTML

Embry-Riddle: *Avion*
http://avion.db.erau.edu

Florida: *The Florida Compass*
http://www.jou.ufl.edu/enews/cmphome.htm

Florida: *The Independent Florida Aligator*
http://www.freenet.ufl.edu/~ifa/

Florida A&M: *Journey* (magazine)
http://wane-leon-mail.scri.fsu.edu/~lpatrick/journey

Franklin and Marshall College: *The College Reporter*
http://www.fandm.edu/StudentLife/Organizations/CollegeReporter/
CollegeReporter.html

Georgia College: *The Colonnade*
http://acs5.gac.peachnet.edu/~colonade/

Hamilton College: *The Spectator*
http://www.hamilton.edu/html/news/studentmedia/spectator/

Harvard: *Student publications*
http://hcs.harvard.edu/

Harvard: *The Salient*
http://www.fierce.net/Salient

Hendrix College: *The Profile*
http://192.131.98.11/Profile/OnlineHomePage.html

Hillsborough Community College: *Hawkeye*
http://www.hcc.cc.fl.us/campus/studpub/hawkeye/hawk.htm

Humboldt State: *The Lumberjack*
http://lumberjack.humboldt.edu

Illinois: *Melvin* (magazine)
http://www.melvin.com/

Illinois: *The Daily Illini*
gopher://vixen.cso.uiuc.edu/11/News/DI

Indiana: *The IU Newspaper*
http://www.indiana.edu/iunews/welcome.html

Iowa State: *Iowa State Daily*
http://www.daily.iastate.edu/

Kansas: *University Daily Kansan*
http://kuhttp.cc.ukans.edu/cwis/UDK/UDKpg1.html

Kansas State: *Kansas State Collegian*
http://www.spub.ksu.edu

Kentucky: *Kentucky Kernel*
http://www.uky.edu/KyKernel

Lehigh: *The Brown and White*
http://www.lehigh.edu/~inbrw/inbrw.html

Louisiana State: *The Daily Reveille*
http://www.lsu.edu/~revedit/index.html

Louisiana Tech: *Tech Talk*
gopher://blick.journ.latech.edu:70/1D-4:2722:%20Tech%20Talk%20

Marin: *The Echo Times*
http://www.marin.cc.ca.us/~shaw/et.html

Marquette: *Marquette Tribune*
http://vinny.csd.mu.edu/tribune/tribune.html

Marshall: *The Parthenon*
http://www.marshall.edu/parthenon/

Massachusetts: *Campus Chronicle*
http://klaatu.oit.umass.edu:80/pubaffs/chronicle/

Mesa Community College: *Mesa Legend*
http://www.mc.maricopa.edu/mesa_legend/

Miami (Oxford, Ohio): *Miami Report*
http://MiaVX1.MUOhio.Edu/~UCMCWIS/NewsBureau/Report

Michigan: *The Michigan Daily*
http://www.pub.umich.edu/daily/index.html

Michigan: *The Monroe Street Journal*
http://www.umich.edu/~msjrnl/

Minnesota: *The Minnesota Daily*
http://www.daily.umn.edu

Missouri: *Maneater*
http://www.phlab.missouri.edu/~maneater/

Missouri: *The Columbia Missourian* (a community newspaper published
by faculty and students)
http://digmo.org

Missouri-Rolla: *Missouri Miner*
http://www.umr.edu:80/~miner/

MIT: *Counterpoint*
http://www.mit.edu:8001/activities/cpt/home.html

MIT: *The Tech*
http://the-tech.mit.edu

Montana: *Montana Kaimin*
http://www.umt.edu/kaimin

Montclair State: *Montclarion*
http://www.montclair.edu/Pages/Montclarion/Montclarion.html

Mt. Holyoke: *College Street Journal*
http://www.mtholyoke.edu:2780/csj/top.html

Nebraska: *Daily Nebraskan*
http://www.unl.edu/DailyNeb/

Nebraska-Omaha: *Gateway*
http://gateway-news.unomaha.edu/gateway/gateway.html

Nevada: *Sagebrush*
http://www.connectus.com/~sgbrush/

New York Polytechnic: *The Fusion*
http://rama.poly.edu/fusion/fusion.html

New York University: *Washington Square News*
http://www.nyu.edu/pages/wsn

North Carolina: *The Daily Tar Heel*
http://www.unc.edu/dth

North Carolina State: *Technician*
http://www2.ncsu.edu/ncsu/stud_pubs/Technician

Northern Illinois: *The Northern Star*
http://www.star.niu.edu

Northern Iowa: *Northern Iowan*
http://www.uni.edu/northia/

North Florida: *Spinnaker*
http://www.unf.edu/groups/spinnaker

Northwestern: *The Daily Northwestern*
http://www.studorg.nwu.edu/daily/

Ohio: *The Bridge Christian*
http://linus.cs.ohiou.edu/~bridge
Ohio: The Post http://132.235.238.184

Ohio State: *The Lantern*
gopher://gopher.acs.ohio-state.edu:70/11/News%20and%20Weather/The%20Lantern

Ohio Wesleyan: *The Transcript*
http://192.68.223.4:8000/transcript/transcr.html

Oklahoma: *The Oklahoma Daily*
http://www.uoknor.edu/okdaily/

Oregon: *Commentator*
http://gladstone.uoregon.edu/~lukeseem/commentator.html

Oregon: *Oregon Daily Emerald* and *Undercurrent*
http://darkwing.uoregon.edu/~heroux/home.html

Pennsylvania: *The Daily Pennsylvanian*
http://www.dp.upenn.edu

Pennsylvania: *Vision*
http://dolphin.upenn.edu/~vision/

Princeton: *Princeton Daily Spigot*
http://www.princeton.edu:80/~spigot/index.html

Rensselaer: *The Polytechnic*
http://www.rpi.edu/dept/union/poly/public_html/polyhome.html

San Francisco State: *Golden Gater*
http://www.journalism.sfsu.edu/www/pubs/gater/gater.htm

San Francisco State: *Prism* (magazine)
http://www.journalism.sfsu.edu/www/pubs/prism/prism.htm

Santa Clara: *The Santa Clara Online*
http://www-tsc.scu.edu/

Santa Rosa Junior College: *The OakLeaf*
http://oakleaf.santarosa.edu/mainmenu/issues/oakleaf.html

Simpson College: *The Simpsonian*
http://storm.simpson.edu/~thesimp

Southern Connecticut State: *Southern News Online*
http://www.scsu-cs.ctstateu.edu/snews/

South Florida: *The Catalyst*
http://www.sar.usf.edu/~catalyst/index.html

Southwest Texas State: *The Daily University Star*
http://www.star.so.swt.edu/0-Star01.html

Stanford: *The Stanford Daily*
http://www-daily.stanford.edu/

Swarthmore: *Phoenix*
http://sccs.swarthmore.edu/org/phoenix/phoenix.html

Syracuse: *Orange Source*
http://source.syr.edu

Temple: *Column*
http://astro.temple.edu/~horus/column/

Temple: *The Temple News*
http://astro.temple.edu/~kate

Tennesee-Knoxville: *The Daily Beacon*
http://beacon-www.asa.utk.edu

Texas: *Tex* (alternative)
http://www.utexas.edu/students/subtex/.web/

Texas: *The Daily Texan*
http://www.utexas.edu/depts/output/www/news.html

Trinity College (Conn.): *Trincoll Journal*
http://www.trincoll.edu/tj/trincolljournal.html

Tufts: *The Observer*
http://www.tufts.edu/~observer

Tufts: *The Tufts Daily*
http://www.tufts.edu/~tdaily

UCLA: *The Daily Bruin*
http://www-paradigm.asucla.ucla.edu

Utah State: *Statesman*
http://cc.usu.edu/~statesman/

Vanderbilt: *The Vanderbilt Hustler*
http://www.vanderbilt.edu/~hustler/index.html

Vassar: *Miscellany News*
http://misc.vassar.edu

Virginia: *The Cavalier Daily*
http://www.virginia.edu/~cavdaily/

Virginia Tech: *Collegiate Times*
   http://www.vt.edu:10021/news/collegiateTimes/ct.html
Wake Forest: *Old Black and Gold*
   http://ogb.wfu.edu
Washington: *The Daily*
   http://www.thedaily.washington.edu
Wayne State: *The South End*
   http://www.southend.wayne.edu
Western Kentucky: *Herald*
   http://www.msc.wku.edu/Info/Herald/heraldol.html
Western Michigan: *The Western Herald*
   http://www.wmich.edu/herald/
Wisconsin: *Online Wisconsin*
   http://journalism.wisc.edu
Wisconsin-Platteville: *Exponent*
   http://www.uwplatt.edu/exponent/
Wooster: *The Wooster Voice Online*
   http://140.103.28.181/
Worchester Polytechnic: *Newspeak*
   http://www.wpi.edu/~newspeak/
Wyoming: *Laramie Online*
   http://www.uwyo.edu/a&s/comm/lns/online.htm
Yale: *Herald*
   http://www.cis.yale.edu/herald/
Yale: *Record*
   http://minerva.cis.yale.edu/~jgfoot/record/rmenu.html
Yale: *The Yale Daily News*
   http://www.yale.edu/ydn/

MAGAZINES

ABCDEFG
   http://www.dakota.net/~pwinn/abcdefg/index.html
Academe This Week
   http://chronicle.merit.edu
Acropolis
   http://www.acropolis.com/acropolis
Advantage NewsMagazine
   http://www.csn.net/~johnhart/newsmag.html

Adventure West
http://www.adventurewest.com

Advertising Age
http://www.adage.com

AE Magazine (Canada)
http://www.io.org/~hideout/ae/ae.html
Aegiss Journal of Professional Knowledge Management
http://www.aegiss.com/journal.htm

Albion Monitor
http://www.monitor.net/monitor/

Alpine World
http://www.sierra.net/alpworld

American Journalism Review
http://www.inform.umd.edu/News/AJR/ajr.html

American Journal of Nursing
http://www.ajn.org

American Prospect
http://epn.org/prospect.html

American Wine
http://www.2way.com/food/wine

America's 4X4 4U (Trucks)
http://www.4x44u.com/pub/k2/am4x44u/4x4.html

Amiga Format
http://www.futurenet.co.uk/computing/amigaformat.html

Amiga Power
http://www.futurenet.co.uk/games/amigapower.html

Amiga Report
http://www.omnipresence.com/Amiga/News/AR/

Amiga Shopper
http://www.futurenet.co.uk/computing/amigashopper.html

Amp (Music)
http://www.mca.com/mca_records/index.html

Amstrad Action
http://www.futurenet.co.uk/computing/amstradaction.html

Angel Exhaust (Poetry)
http://www.offworld.org/angel-exhaust/Welcome.html

Antiques and the Arts Weekly
http://www.connix.com:80/thebee/aweb/aa.htm

APICS—The Performance Advantage
http://lionhrtpub.com/APICS.html

Ariga (Israeli)
  http://www.ariga.com
Armchair Scientist
  http://www.areacom.it/html/ita/loris/armchair.html
Art Bin
  http://aristotle.algonet.se/artbin/
ArtDirect
  http://artdirect.com/home.html
Arts Reach
  http://www.artswire.org/Artswire/ArtsReach/home.html
Ascending Node
  http://seds.lpl.arizona.edu/nodes/ass_node.html
Asia Inc.
  http://www.asia-inc.com
Atlantic Monthly
  http://www.theatlantic.com
Auer Grafikdienst
  http://www.auer.magnet.at/auer/
Australian Finance Review
  http://www.afr.com.au/index.html
Australian Observer
  http://www.ozemail.com.au/observer/
Australian PC User
  http://www.pcuser.com.au
Australian Personal Computer
  http://www.com.au/apc
Austria Culture Net
  http://www.austriaculture.net
Axcess
  http://www.internex.net/axcess
Back Channel
  http://www.commercepark.com/AAAA/bc.html
Baguette
  http://www.mmania.com/
Basement (Music, literature)
  http://www.ios.com/~dizzyman/
Basilisk
  http://swerve.basilisk.com/
BBS Magazine
  http://www.bbsmag.com

Beatrice
   http://www.primenet.com/~grifter/beatrice.html
Bidding on Bay Street (Canada)
   http://www.eucanect.com/investments/bayst.html
Blood Alley
   http://www.vannet.com/vanecho/magazine.htm
Blue Penny Quarterly
   http://ebbs.english.vt.edu/olp/bpq/front-page.html
Boardwatch
   http://www.boardwatch.com
Boat Drinks
   http://www.boatdrinks.com/clients/windward/default.html
Boston Book Review
   http://www.bookwire.com/bbr/bbr-home.html
Breed Apart (Greyhounds)
   http://www.pcix.com/abap/index.html
Brew
   http://RealBeer.com/brew/
Bright Lights Film Journal
   http://www.crl.com/~gsamuel/bright.html
Builder
   http://www.builderonline.com
Business to Business
   (Ontario)http://www.tcn.net/~bus2bus/welcome.html
Business Traveler
   http://www.biztravel.com/guide/
Buzz
   http://www.buzzmag.com/buzz/
BuzzNet
   http://www.hooked.net:80/buzznet/
Byte
   http://www.byte.com/byte.htm
Caffeine Magazine
   http://www.hallucinet.com/caffeine
Callaloo (African-American)
   http://muse.jhu.edu/journals/callaloo/index.html
Canadian Medical Association Journal
   http://hpb1.hwc.ca:8400/
Carbon 14 (New Age)
   http://www.rsabbs.com/carbon14/

Career Magazine
   http://www.careermag.com/careermag/index.html

Car Magazine (Britain)
   http://www.mpn.com/eol/car/

CAUSE/EFFECT
   http://cause-www.colorado.edu/cause-effect/cause-effect.html

CD-ROM Today
   http://www.futurenet.co.uk/computing/cdromtoday.html

Celebrator
   http://realbeer.com:80/celebrator/

Century
   http://www.supranet.com/century/

Change Magazine
   http://www.imaja.com/imaja/change

Chaos Control
   http://www.std.com/obi/Zines/Chaos.Control/chaos.html

Chimney Professionals
   http://www.ultranet.com/biz/chimneys/

China Business Journal
   http://silkroute.com/silkroute/news/cbj/cbj.html

Choir
   http://www.greencart.com/choir/index.html

Christian Computing
   http://www.website.net/~ccmag/

CIO
   http://www.cio.com/CIO

Circuit Traces
   http://vanbc.wimsey.com/~chrish/

CityLife Brussels
   http://www.cityeurope.com/

CLiCK
   http://www.click.com.au

CMC
   http://sunsite.unc.edu/cmc/mag/current/toc.html

Cobb Group
   http://www.zdnet.com/~cobb

Cocktail
   http://www.italia.com/cocktail/

Coloquio
   http://www.clark.net/pub/jgbustam/coloquio/coloquio.html

Columbia Journalism Review
http://www.cjr.org/

Columbus Sports and Fitness Magazine
http://www.columbuspages.com/sportfitmag/

Coming Soon
http://www.megatoon.com/~t15/

Commodore Format
http://www.futurenet.co.uk/computing/commodoreformat.html

Commodore Hacking
http://www.msen.com/~brain/chacking.html

Communication Arts
http://www.commarts.com

CommunicationsWeek
http://techweb.cmp.com:80/techweb/cw/current

Competitor (Sports)
http://competitor.com/

Computer Buyer Magazine
http://www.giaco.com

Computer Gaming World
http://www.gamingworld.ziff.com/~gaming/

Computer Life
http://www.zdnet.com/~complife

Computer Mediated Communication
http://www.rpi.edu/~decemj/cmc/mag/current/toc.html

Computer Reseller News
http://techweb.cmp.com:80/techweb/crn/current

Computer Retail Week
http://techweb.cmp.com:80/techweb/crw/current

Computer Shopper
http://www.shopper.ziff.com/~cshopper/textonly.html

Computing
http://www.mpn.com/vnu/ctg/latest/

Concious Choice
http://www.consciouschoice.com/Home.html

Conde Nast Traveler
http://www.cntraveler.com

ContextXXI
http://stud2.tuwien.ac.at/~e8426940/context.html

Contra Mundum
http://www.wavefront.com/~contra_m/cm/cm.html

Cornell Law Review
   http://www.law.cornell.edu:80/clr/clr.htm

Creative Loafing
   http://web.cc.emory.edu/CL/loafing.html

Critical Mass
   http://fas.sfu.ca/comm/c-mass/c-mass.html

Crossroads (Computer)
   http://info.acm.org/crossroads/

Cross Stitch Collection
   http://www.futurenet.co.uk/crafts/crossstitchcoll.html

Cross Stitcher
   http://www.futurenet.co.uk/crafts/crossstitcher.html

Current
   http://artswire.org/Artswire/www/current.html

Current (Broadcasting)
   http://www.current.org

Cyanosis (Art)
   http://www2.system-zero.com/syszero/cyanosis/cyanosis.html

CyberKids
   http://www.mtlake.com/cyberkids/

Cyberkind
   http://sunsite.unc.edu/shannon/ckind/title.html

CyberSpokesman
   http://tecnet2.jcte.jcs.mil:8000/cybrspke/cybrspke.html

Cycling Plus
   http://www.futurenet.co.uk/outdoors/cyclingplus.html

Dallas Child
   http://www.pic.net/uniloc/child/index.html

Dance Ink
   http://www.webcom.com/~ink/welcome.html

Datamation
   http://www.datamation.com

d.Comm
   http://www.d-comm.com/

Delicious
   http://www.newhope.com/public/delicious/D!_home.html

Dell Horoscope Magazine
   http://www.bdd.com/horo1/bddhoro1.cgi

Denver's Mile High Magazine
http://www.5280pub.com 5280:

Der Spiegel (Germany)
http://www.spiegel.de

Desktop Publishing
http://www.demon.co.uk/cyber/dp/dp.html

Digitale
http://www.umn.edu/nlhome/m447/reinb001/digi/digitale.html

Discover
http://www.enews.com:80/magazines/discover/

Dive Destinations
http://www.atonet.com/dive/

Downstate Story
http://www.wiu.bgu.edu/users/mfgeh/dss

Echo (Southwest)
http://www.comeout.com/echo

EcoLink
http://www.envirolink.org/EcoLink

Edge Magazine
http://www.edgeonline.com/edge/edgemag.htm

Edifice of Writing
http://www-leland.stanford.edu/~lmgorbea/

Editor & Publisher
http://www.mediainfo.com/edpub/ep/index.htm

Educom Review
http://educom.edu/

E Law: Murdoch University Electronic Journal of Law
http://portia.murdoch.edu.au/libweb/Elib/Jnls/Murdoch/Elaw/elaw.html

Electric Pages
http://www.electric-pages.com/

Electronic Buyers' News
http://techweb.cmp.com:80/techweb/ebn/current

Electronic Engineering Times
http://techweb.cmp.com:80/techweb/eet/current

Electronic Gaming Monthly
http://www.nuke.com

Electronic Revenge
http://pobox.com/slt/ Sam Johnson's

Electronic Urban Report
   http://www.LeeBailey.com/eur.html
Entertainment Weekly
   http://www.timeinc.com/ew/
Enterzone
   http://enterzone.berkeley.edu/enterzone.html
Entrepreneur Weekly
   http://www.eweekly.com/
Environment Business (Britain)
   http://www.pavilion.co.uk/vinet/ifi/ebm/
Epicurious
   http://www.epicurious.com
Euphony
   http://imagineer.com/euphony/
Everton's Genealogical Helper
   http://www.xmission.com/~jayhall/ghonline.html
Exposure (Art)
   http://www.deltanet.com/cerro-villa/exposure/exp_pg1.html
Extra! (Media)
   http://www.fair.org/fair/extra/
Eye Weekly
   http://www.interlog.com/eye
Families and Disabilities News
   http://kuhttp.cc.ukans.edu/cwis/units/LSI/b/beachhp.html
Families USA
   http://epn.org/families.html
Family World
   http://family.com
Farm Journal
   http://www.FarmJournal.com/
Faulkner's cc:Browser
   http://www.faulkner.com
Federal Communications Law Journal
   http://www.law.indiana.edu/fclj/fclj.html
Feed
   http://www.feedmag.com
Filters
   http://www.teleport.com/~mattr/manifesto.htm
Financial Mail (South Africa)
   http://www.atd.co.za/fm

Financial Planning On-line
http://www.tisny.com/fponline

Firehorse
http://www.peg.apc.org/~firehorse/welcome.html

First Perspective (Canada)
http://www.mbnet.mb.ca/firstper

Fix
http://www.easynet.co.uk/fix/fix.htm

Fly Fishing Online
http://www.flyfishing-online.com/netscape/news/index.html

F MagZine (Canada)
http://www.musicwest.com/fmag

Focus
http://www.netsurf.com/nsf/index.html

Fortune
http://pathfinder.com/fortune

Foster Parent News
http://www.worldaccess.com/~clg46/news.htm

Freaker
http://conan.ids.net/starbridge/freaker/

FreePress (Prescott, Ariz.)
http://www.bslnet.com/accounts/frepress/www/index.html

FrogMag (French)
http://www.princeton.edu/Frogmag

From Now On (Education)
http://www.pacificrim.net/~mckenzie/

Front Page (German)
http://www.techno.de/frontpage/index.html

Fryburger (Fiction)
http://www.uni-freiburg.de/borsch/fryburger/fryburger.html

Future Music
http://www.futurenet.co.uk/music/futuremusic.html

Game Report
http://www.wolfe.net/~peter/tgr/

Gamer's Zone
http://www.worldvillage.com/wv/gamezone/html/gamezone.htm

Games Domain Review
http://wcl-rs.bham.ac.uk/gdreview

GamesMaster
http://www.futurenet.co.uk/games/gamesmaster.html

GameWave
    http://wantree.com.au/gamewave
George
    http://www.georgemag.com
Global Link (Music)
    http://kiwi.futuris.net/rw/motw/
Global Monitor
    http://www.globalx.net/monitor/
Global Network News
    http://gnn.com/GNNhome.html
Glow (Art)
    http://www.vyne.com/glow/index.html
GolfNetwork
    http://cigww3.ecom.dec.com/mcs/golfnet/mmenu.html
Good Woodworking
    http://www.futurenet.co.uk/crafts/goodwoodworking.html
Government Technology
    http://www.govtech.net/
Green Cart (Art)
    http://www.greencart.com//greencart/maincontent.html
Growing Edge
    http://www.teleport.com/~tomalex/GE.HTML
Gruene Street Journal
    http://www-bprc.mps.ohio-state.edu/cgi-bin/hpp/gruene.html
Guided Waters (Fishing)
    http://guidedwaters.com/flyfishing
HalluciNet (Music)
    http://www.hallucinet.com
Harvard Computer Review
    http://hcs.harvard.edu/~hcr/
Hastings Women's Law Journal
    http://www.uchastings.edu/womenslj/womenslj.html
Hebdo (French)
    http://www.hebdo.ch/
Hemmings Motor News
    http://maple.sover.net/~hemmings/hmn.html
Heritage (Christian)
    http://www.fni.com/heritage/
Heritage Post (Canada)
    http://heritage.excite.sfu.ca/hpost.html

Home Business Review
   http://www.tab.com/Home.Business
HomePC
   http://techweb.cmp.com:80/techweb/hpc/current
Hootenanny
   http://web.syr.edu/~drkeith/hootenanny.html
Horses
   http://www.connix.com:80/thebee/hweb/horses.htm
hp-ux/usr
   http://www.interex.org/hpuxusr/
Human Rights Brief
   http://sray.wcl.american.edu/pub/journals/hmnrghts.htm
Hungry Mind Review
   http://www.iw.net/~mind/Review
Hyper@ctive
   http://hyperactive.com/games/
HyperZine
   http://www.hyperzine.com/hypznhm.html
IceNEWS
   http://www.tiac.net/users/wcrawfor/icenews/
Ideal Times (Business)
   http://clever.net/prestige/ideal.htm
Ideas DIGest
   http://www.ideas.wis.net/
Imagination
   http://193.140.195.221/imagination/
ImprovisAsians (Asian American)
   http://www.wp.com/horiuchi/improv1.html
Index on Censorship
   http://www.oneworld.org/index_oc/
Indiana Journal of Global Legal Studies
   http://www.law.indiana.edu/glsj/glsj.html
Indianapolis Monthly
   http://www.iquest.net/indymonthly
Indy Car Racing
   http://www.icr.com
Infobahn
   http://www.postmodern.com/
InfoNation
   http://www.info-nation.com

Informatie & informatiebeleid (Dutch)
http://www.nic.surfnet.nl/cram/i&i/

InformationWeek
http://techweb.cmp.com:80/techweb/iw/current

Informatiques
http://techweb.cmp.com:80/techweb//corporate/international/
informatique.html

In Motion Magazine
http://www.inmotionmagazine.com

Inter@ctive Week
http://www.zdnet.com/~intweek

InfoWorld
http://www2.internet.net/stores/infoworld/index.html

Initiatives Online
http://web.wpi.org/uetc/initidx.htm

Inquisitor
http://www.echonyc.com/~xixax/Mediarama/Inquisitor/

Intelligent Gamer
http://igonline.escape.com/

Interact
http://www.interex.org/interact/

InteractiveAge
http://techweb.cmp.com:80/techweb/ia/current

International (Computers)
http://techweb.cmp.com:80/techweb/cwi/current

International Teletimes
http://www.wimsey.com/teletimes/teletimes_home_page.html

Internaut
http://www.zilker.net/users/internaut/index.html

Internet Australasia
http://www.world.net/magazine/

Internet.Com (Spanish)
http://www.colomsat.net.co/internetcom

Internet Herald
http://server.berkeley.edu/herald

Internet Life
http://www.zdnet.com/zdil ZD

Internet Magazine
http://http://www.emap.co.uk/comp/magazines/internet/

Internet Week
  http://www.phillips.com/pbi/iw/index.html
Internet World
  http://www.mecklerweb.com/mags/iw/iwhome.htm
Interregnum
  http://www.tiac.net/users/maranci/index.html
InterText E-zine
  http://www.etext.org/Zines/InterText/
I/O Magazine
  http://www.mother.com/iomag/Welcome.html
Ion Science
  http://www.injersey.com/Media/IonSci/
Issachar Journal (Christian)
  http://www.iquest.net/visionweb/journal.html
IT Informer
  http://www.keyway.net/mmp/
iWORLD
  http://www.mecklerweb.com/netday/newsmenu.htm
Japanese Technology Business
  http://web.kyoto-inet.or.jp/people/mattm/
Jazz Online
  http://www.flightpath.com/Clients/JazzOnln/
Journal for Patriotic Justice in America
  http://www.eskimo.com/~hmcom/4/a.html
Journal of Electronic Defense
  http://www.jedefense.com/jed.html
Journal of Gender and The Law
  http://sray.wcl.american.edu/pub/journals/gender.htm
Journal of International Law and Policy
  http://sray.wcl.american.edu/pub/journals/ilj.htm
Journal of Online Law
  http://www.law.cornell.edu/jol/jol.table.html
Kagyu Life International (Buddhist)
  http://users.aimnet.com/~kclsf/kl.htm
Kansas City
  http://www.fileshop.com/infozine/ infoZine
Kennedy Market Letter
  http://www2.ari.net/home/kmletter/

Korea Economic Weekly
http://eco.ked.co.kr/h-kew.html

Kulttuurivihkot (Finnish)
http://www.clinet.fi/~lyhty/vihkot.html

kulturCHOCK! (Swedish-American)
http://www.webcom.com/~eha/kchock.html

LAN on the Web
http://www.lanmag.com

LAN Times
http://www.wcmh.com/lantimes

La Recherche (French)
http://daec.obspm.fr/larecherche/

Law Notes (Canada)
http://www.discribe.ca/murco/MurCo.html

Legal Automation and Internet Review
http://www.law.utexas.edu/lair/lair.html

Legal Information Institute
http://www.law.cornell.edu/

Let's Fly & Cruise
http://www.digimark.net/rec-travel/tagents/lets-fly-
cruise/index.html

Life
http://www.pathfinder.com/@@3bDsAgAAAAAAGzz/Life/
lifehome.html

L'Independant (Quebec)
http://www.cam.org/~paslap/ajiq/independant.html

Link
http://metro.turnpike.net/metro/meulie/link0.htm

Linn's Stamp News
http://www.best.com:80/~linns/

Linux Gazette
http://www.tenn.com/fiskhtml/gazette_toc.html

Linux Journal
http://www.ssc.com/lj/index.html

LINX-LUG Information News Exchange
http://www.sims.net/organizations/linx/linxhome.html

Listen Up
http://www.interport.net/~anthem/

Living Large Network
http://www.lln.com/

Living Poets
   http://dougal.derby.ac.uk/lpoets/

Lumpen
   http://www.lumpen.com/lumpen/

Mac/Chicago Online
   http://www.macchicago.com/home/

MacFormat
   http://www.futurenet.co.uk/computing/macformat.html

MacSense
   http://ats4.colorado.edu/OLM/MacSense/MS.html

MacTech
   http://www.mactech.com

MacUser
   http://www.macuser.ziff.com/~macuser/

MacWeek
   http://www.ziff.com/~macweek/

MacWorld
   http://www.macworld.com

Maine Antique Digest
   http://www.maine.com/mad

Max CD ROM
   http://techweb.cmp.com:80/techweb/max/current

Media Bypass
   http://www.ionet.net/~ordway/

MediaCentral
   http://www.mediacentral.com

Mediator (Europe)
   http://mediator.pira.co.uk/index.html

MediaTribe
   http://www.cs.concordia.ca/vlib/mtribe/mtribe.html

Medical Reporter
   http://www.dash.com/netro/nwx/tmr/tmr.html

Merlin's Web (Magic)
   http://www.swifty.com/MW/toc.html

MESH: Inside Cyberspace
   http://www.albany.globalone.net/theMESH/

Michigan Telecommunications and Technology Law Review
   http://www.umich.edu/~umlaw/mttlr.html

Microwave Journal
   http://www.mwjournal.com/mwj.html

Midwest Today
  http://www.midtod.com
Mississippi Review
  http://www.usm.edu/usmhburg/lib_arts/english/cen4writers/
  c4wmain.html
Mobilis
  http://www.volksware.com/mobilis
Money
  http://pathfinder.com/money
Mother Jones
  http://www.mojones.com
Motive
  http://granite.sentex.net:80/motive/index.html
Motorcycle
  http://www.motorcycle.com
Motorcycle Shopper
  http://www.mshopper.eurografix.com
Mountain Biking Pro
  http://www.futurenet.co.uk/outdoors/mtbpro.html
MultiMedia World
  http://www.mmworld.com
Munich Found
  http://www.isgi.de/MunichFound/
Muse
  http://www.hyperlink.com/muse/
Museos
  http://www.cmact.com/publicwww/museos/museums.htm
Muse Week
  http://jefferson.fairfield.com/cyberspacecafe/museweek.html
Mushing
  http://www.polarnet.com/Users/Mushing/
Mutual Funds Magazine
  http://www.mfmag.com/aam
NASDAQ Financial Executive Journal
  http://www.law.cornell.edu/nasdaq/nasdtoc.html
National Computer Tectonics
  http://awa.com/nct/
National Law Journal
  http://www.ljextra.com/nlj/

Nature
   http://www.nature.com
Needlecraft
   http://www.futurenet.co.uk/crafts/needlecraft.html
.net
   http://www.futurenet.co.uk/netmag/net.html
Net Gazette
   http://www.teleport.com/~stevew/index.html
NetGuide
   http://techweb.cmp.com:80/techweb/ng/current
Net Literary Journal
   http://www.webcom.com/~netjourn/welcome.html
Netsurfer Digest
   http://www.netsurf.com/nsd/
NetWatch
   http://www.pulver.com/netwatch
NetWatchers
   http://www.ionet.net/~mdyer/netwatch.html
Network Computing
   http://techweb.cmp.com:80/techweb/nc/current
Network Science
   http://www.awod.com/netsci/
Network World
   http://www.nwfusion.com/
New American (Political)
   http://www.primenet.com/~tevans/newamericanindex.html
New England Organist
   http://www.cybercom.net/~tneorg
NewMedia Magazine
   http://www.hyperstand.com/
New Reformation Review
   http://www.mindspring.com/~krwatson/nrr/
New Republic
   http://www.enews.com/magazines/tnr/
Newscan (Canada)
   http://www.nstn.ca/wshdc/newscan.html
New Space
   http://www.newspace.com/publications/newsletter/newsindex.html

NewType
    http://WWW.newtype.com/NewType/
NeWWW
    http://grafton.dartmouth.edu:8023/
New Zealand InfoTech Weekly
    http://www.infotech.co.nz
Next (Chinese)
    http://www.next.com.hk/next
NextAge
    http://www.geopages.com/WestHollywood/2125/
NIC News
    http://www.washington.edu/nic-news/
Nightclub and Bar Magazine
    http://www.inst.com:80/ncb/Welcome.html
Nikkei Business Press
    http://www.nikkeibp.co.jp/english.html
Northern Miner
    http://www.southam.com/northernminer/
NorthWest Aviation Trader
    http://www.direct.ca:80/flying/
NRC Handelsblad (Netherlands)
    http://www.nrc.nl/Web/vp.html
Ocean Navigator
    http://www.sailnet.com/onav/index.htm
OEM Magazine
    http://techweb.cmp.com:80/techweb/oem/current
Offshore Investment Magazine
    http://www.offshoreinvestment.com/offshore/index.html
Oldenburger Stachel (German)
    http://www.informatik.uni-oldenburg.de/~muh/Stachel/
Old Farmer's Almanac
    http://www.nj.com/weather
Omphalos (Fiction)
    http://thule.mt.cs.cmu.edu:8001/sf-clearing-house/zines/omphalos/
OneEurope
    http://www.informatik.rwth-aachen.de/AEGEE/oneEurope/
On Line Design
    http://www.cea.edu/online.design/

Online Educator
http://www.cris.com/~felixg/OE/OEWELCOME.html

Online Journal of Ethics
http://condor.depaul.edu/ethics/ethg1.html

Online Magazine
http://www.online-magazine.com

Online World Monitor
http://login.eunet.no/~presno/monitor.html

On the Issues
http://mosaic.echonyc.com/~onissues/index.htm

Open Computing
http://www.wcmh.com/oc

Open Scroll
http://www.hooked.net:80/users/toconnor/index.html

Ora.Com
http://www.ora.com/gnn/bus/ora/features/index.html

OR/MS Today
http://lionhrtpub.com

OS/2 Connect
http://warp.eecs.berkeley.edu/os2

Outdoor Nova Scotia
http://www.isisnet.com/haligonian/outdoor/

Outside Online
http://www.starwave.com/outside/online

Oyster Boy Review
http://ruby.ils.unc.edu/oyster_boy/

Paine News
http://www.mindspring.com/~cudworth/PAINENEWS.html

Pajavasara (Finnish)
http://www.mediakylpyla.hel.fi/pajavasara

Paris Review
http://www.voyagerco.com/PR/p.toc.html

Passport (San Antonio)
http://www.gadsby.com/passport

PAWWS (Financial)
http://pawws.secapl.com

PC Answers
http://www.futurenet.co.uk/computing/pcanswers.html

PCAttack
   http://www.futurenet.co.uk/computing/PCAttack.html
PC Computing
   http://www.zdnet.com/~pccomp
PC Format
   http://www.futurenet.co.uk/computing/pcformat.html
PC Gamer
   http://www.futurenet.co.uk/computing/pcgamer.html
PC Magazine
   http://www.pcmag.ziff.com/~pcmag/
PC Multimedia Entertainment
   http://mortimer.com/users/pcme/pcme.htm
PC Plus
   http://www.futurenet.co.uk/computing/pcplus.html
PC Review Magazine (Britain)
   http://www.mpn.com/eol/pcr/pcrhome.htm
PC Week
   http://www.pcweek.ziff.com/~pcweek/
PC World
   http://www.pcworld.com
Peaks (Montana)
   http://cpmt.cyberport.net:80/peaks/
Pen and Sword
   http://www.rahul.net/jag/
Pen-Based Computing
   http://WWW.VOLKSWARE.COM/pbc/promo.htm
Penthouse
   http://www.penthousemag.com
People
   http://www.timeinc.com/people/
Phoenix
   http://www.gartland.com/phoenix/index.html
Photo Electronic Imaging
   http://www.novalink.com/pei.html
Photon
   http://www.scotborders.co.uk/photon/
Plain Truth (Religious)
   http://www.wcg.org/pt/index.htm

Planeta Platica
   http://www.greenbuilder.com/mader/planeta/planeta_current.html
Planning Commissioners Journal
   http://www.webcom.com/~pcj/welcome.html
Plant Engineer
   http://www.iac.net:80/isis/ishome.html
Playbill
   http://www.webcom.com/~broadway/
Playboy
   http://www.playboy.com
Plexus
   http://www.interport.net/~plexus/
Point (South Carolina)
   http://www.cris.com/~Scpoint/
PoliticsUSA
   http://PoliticsUSA.com
Popular Mechanics
   http://popularmechanics.com
Portico (Some Spanish)
   http://www.gn.apc.org/redgrround
Princeton Progressive Review
   http://www.princeton.edu:80/~progrev/index.html
Principle (Political)
   http://www.brown.edu/Students/Brown_College_Democrats/
   principle.html
Private Eye (Satire)
   http://www.intervid.co.uk/intervid/eye/gateway.html
Professional Boatbuilder
   http://media2.hypernet.com/PROBOAT/pbb.htm
Progression
   http://www.gold.net/users/ex14/
Progressive
   http://www.igc.apc.org/igc/www.news.html
Progressive Farmer
   http://www.pathfinder.com/PF
Progressive Populist
   http://www.eden.com/~reporter
Progressive Review
   http://emporium.turnpike.net/P/ProRev/index.html

Pro-Life News
   http://www.pitt.edu/~stfst/pln/AboutPLN.html
Promethean Journal
   http://www.cts.com/~andym/lexia/pj/
Q (San Francisco)
   http://www.qsanfrancisco.com
Quill
   http://town.hall.org/places/spj/quill.html
Quincaillerie Materiaux
   http://www.cam.org/~valeman/index.html
Quintessenz (Austria)
   http://www.netsphere.co.at/netsphere/
Radio Resistor's Bulletin
   http://www.hear.com/rw/feature/rrb.html
React
   http://www.react.com
Red Dog Journal
   http://www.indirect.com/user/informa/reddog.html
Regards (French)
   http://www.regards.fr/
REVelation
   http://loft-gw.zone.org/evolution/home.html
Richmond Journal of Law and Technology
   http://www.urich.edu/~jolt
Ride! (Equestrian)
   http://www.wsmith.com/ride/ride!mag.htm
RootsWorld
   http://www.rootsworld.com/rw/
Rules and Regulations in Russia: Russian Business Law Journal
   http://www.spb.su/rulesreg/index.html
SalesDoctors
   http://salesdoctors.com
San Diego Magazine
   http://www.sandiego-online.com/
Scarlet Threaded Web
   http://194.72.60.96/www/pwf/holmes.htm
Scholastic
   http://scholastic.com:2005
Science and the Environment
   http://www.voyagepub.com/publish/voyage.htm

Scientific Computing and Automation
http://gordonpub.loyola.edu/

Scientific Computing World (Europe)
http://www.ioppublishing.com/Mags/SCW/index.html

Scout Report
http://rs.internic.net/scout_report-index.html

Scripture Studies
http://www.kaiwan.com/~ssper/sstdys.html

SCUBA World
http://freepubs.bucc.co.uk/SCUBA/index.html

Sea (Boating)
http://www.gsn.com/sea.htm

Security Online
http://www.cityscape.co.uk/users/hl03/index.html

Sega Power
http://www.futurenet.co.uk/games/segapower.html

Sejmik Samorzadowy (Poland)
http://sejmik/wyd_sejm/sej_sam/sejm_95.htm

Self-Help Psychology
http://www.well.com/user/selfhelp/

Seulemonde
http://nosferatu.cas.usf.edu/journal/index.html

SGA Goldstar Research (Financial)
http://sgagoldstar.com/sga/

Shadow (Young Adults)
http://grimmy.santarosa.edu/~tmurphy/shadow.html

Shift Magazine (Canada)
http://www.shift.com/shift.home

Shoestring Travel
http://metro.turnpike.net/eadler/index.html

Sight
http://www.sightphoto.com/photo.html

SIMBA Media Daily
http://www.mecklerweb.com/simba/internet.htm

Sleeping Dog
http://cuboulder.colorado.edu/FineArt/FineArts.html

Social Cafe
http://www.social.com/social/index.html

So It Goes (Poetry)
http://www.pitt.edu/~soitgoes/index.html

Soldiers Magazine
   http://www.redstone.army.mil/soldiers/home.html
SoundOut (Music)
   http://www.tmn.com/0h/Community/juechi/soundout.html
South Florida
   http://sobe.com/sfl
Sports Illustrated
   http://www.timeinc.com/si/
Stanford Law and Policy Review
   http://www-leland.stanford.edu/group/SLPR/
Stellar Business
   http://corp.tig.com/stellar/global/index.html
ST Format
   http://www.futurenet.co.uk/computing/stformat.html
Stick
   http://www.vpm.com/tti/index.html
Streetsound
   http://www.streetsound.com/zone/
Strobe
   http://www.iuma.com/strobe/
Student.Net
   http://www.student.net
Style
   http://www.papermag/com
SunWorld
   http://www.sun.com:80/sunworldonline/
SuperPlay
   http://www.futurenet.co.uk/games/superplay.html
TalkBack
   http://math240.lehman.cuny.edu/talkback
T@P Online
   http://www.taponline.com
Taxi
   http://www.pi.se/taxi
Technology Access
   http://nbn.nbn.com/tar/
Technology Review
   http://web.mit.edu/techreview/www

Telecine
   http://www.rtvf.nwu.edu/Omnibus/TelecineTOC.html
Telecommunications
   http://www.telecoms-mag.com/tcs.html
Telemanagement (Canada)
   http://www.angustel.ca/tm.html
Texture
   http://catalog.com/texture/texture.htm
The Journal (Substance abuse)
   http://www.arf.org/Intropage.html
The Net
   http://www.thenet-usa.com
The New Democrat
   http://www.dlcppi.org/tnd.htm
Thesis (Commentary)
   http://www.hyperlink.com/thesis/
Think
   http://wheel.dcn.davis.ca.us/~csandvig/think/homepage.html
This Old House
   http://www.pathfinder.com/@@Fo*ddJEUpgEAQE1D/TOH/
TidBITS
   http://www.dartmouth.edu/pages/TidBITS/TidBITS.html
TikiZine
   http://uxa.cso.uiuc.edu/~dsk33593/tikizine/
TIME
   http://www.timeinc.com/time/magazine/magazine.html
Time Out (London)
   http://www.timeout.co.uk
Tokyo Journal
   http://www.iac.co.jp/tj/
TOTAL!
   http://www.futurenet.co.uk/games/total.html
Total Guitar
   http://www.futurenet.co.uk/music/totalguitar.html
Total New York
   http://www.totalny.com
Trakker
   http:/regina.ism.ca/trakker/index.htm

TravelAssist
http://travelassist.com/mag/mag_home.html

TravelGram
http://www.csn.net/~johnhart/travgram.html

Tristero (Political)
http://mars.superlink.net/user/cristoph/

TV-Today (German)
http://www.tv.today.de/

Twentieth Century Watch (Religious)
http://www.cgi.org/cgi/watch/watch.htm

U (College Magazine)
http://www.umagazine.com

Ultimate Future Games
http://www.futurenet.co.uk/games/ultimate.html

Uncommon Sense (Political)
http://www.geopages.com/sunsetstrip/1168

UniScience
http://199.44.59.40/unisci/

UnixWorld Online
http://www.wcmh.com/uworld/

Upper Midwest Travel & Adventure Guide
http://www.execpc.com/~midwest

Urban Desires
http://desires.com/

U.S. News & World Report
http://www.usnews.com

U.S. Scanner News
http://www.pacifier.com/~ussn

U.S. Water News
http://www.mother.com/uswaternews/

Utne Reader
http://www.utne.com

U-Turn (Christian)
http://www.tkc.com/tkc/uturn.htm

VAR Business
http://techweb.cmp.com:80/techweb/vb/current

Veckans Affaerer (Swedish)
http://www.bonnier.se/va/ettan.html

Vermont Life
http://www.cit.state.vt.us/vtlife/index.htm

Vibe (Music)
http://www.timeinc.com/vibe/

Video Game Advisor
http://www.vgadvisor.com

Videomaker
http://www.videomaker.com

Villánova Information Law Chronicle
http://ming.law.vill.edu/vill.info.l.chron/

Virtual Entrepreneur
http://emporium.turnpike.net/B/bizopp/index.html

Virtual Garden
http://www.timeinc.com/vg/Welcome/welcome.html

Virtual Mirror
http://mirror.wwa.com/mirror/

Virtual Pathways (Backpacking)
http://edge.edge.net/~jhbryan/virtual_pathways.html

Voiceworks (Australia)
http://ip7.cs.monash.edu.au:4000/vworks.html

Washington
http://fivash.com/

Washington CEO
http://fivash.com/ceo/toc.htm

Washingtonian
http://www.infi.net/washmag/

Washington Ripple
http://nimue.wustl.edu/~ripple/

Washington Weekly
http://dolphin.gulf.net/

Way Ahead (Horse Racing)
http://www.wayahead.com

WebDallas
http://www.computek.net/dynamic/webdallas/webdal.html

Web Developer's Journal
http://www.awa.com/nct/software/eleclead.html

Web Digest for Marketers
http://www.advert.com/wdfm.wdfm.html

Web Journal of Current Legal Issues
http://www.ncl.ac.uk/~nlawwww/

WebMaster
http://www.cio.com/WebMaster

Web Review
   http://gnn.com/wr
WEBster
   http://www.tgc.com/webster.html
WEBsurf
   http://www.crl.com/~whisper/
Web Travel Review
   http://webtravel.org/webtravel/
Week (British)
   http://metrotel.co.uk/theweek/
Westcoast Families
   http://www.vannet.com/WCF/
West's Legal News
   http://www.westpub.com/lnot
What's On Tonite
   http://tvnet.com/WhatsOnTonite/
Who's Marketing Online
   http://www.mindspring.com/~dmonline/WMO.html
Wiener/Basta (Vienna, Austria)
   http://www.ping.at/wiener/
WindoWatch
   http://www.channel1.com/users/winwatch/WindoWatch.html
Windows Magazine
   http://techweb.cmp.com:80/techweb/wm/current
Windows Sources
   http://www.zdnet.com/~wsources
Wine and Dine
   http://www.limitless.co.uk/winedine/
Wired
   http://www.hotwired.com/
WirtschaftsWoche (Austrian)
   http://www.wirtschaftswoche.co.at/wirtschaftswoche/
Wochenpost (German)
   http://www.wochenpost.de/
Word
   http://www.word.com
World3
   http://la.COMMERCE.COM:80/world3/
!WOW!
   http://www.dorsai.org/~tristan/MAG

WP Mac News
   http://www.novell.com:80/SalesMkt/mac/
WWW Virtual Library: Law
   http://www.law.indiana.edu/law/lawindex.html
X Advisor
   http://landru.unx.com/DD/advisor/index.shtml

NEWS SERVICES

Africa Online
   http://www.AfricaOnline.com/AfricaOnline/newsstand.html
AfricaUpdate
   http://neal.ctstateu.edu/history/africa_update/africa_update.html
American Cybercasting (e-mail)
   http://www.americast.com/
American News Service
   http://www.sover.net/~ans
American Reporter
   http://www.newshare.com/Reporter/today.html
Ansa (Italy)
   http://www.ansa.it
Arabic Electronic Mail Journal
   http://www.ibmpcug.co.uk/~ajournal/
Arab Electronic Mail Journal
   http://www.ibmpcug.co.uk/~ajournal/
Associated Press—No service of its own but it is included in many
   online newspapers.
Athens News Agency
   http://www.forthnet.gr/ape/
Australian News Briefs
   http://onthenet.com.au/~thomast/anb/
Australian News Reports
   http://australia-online.com/anr.html
Austrian Press Agency
   http://www.apa.co.at/
Baltic News Service
   http://www.bns.ee
Baltics Online
   http://www.viabalt.ee/News/

Canada NewsWire
   http://www.newswire.ca/
Canadian Corporate NewsNet
   http://www.cdn-news.com
Canadian Press
   http://www.xe.com/canpress/
Central Europe Today
   http://www.eunet.cz/
Central News Agency (Taiwan)
   http://www.sinanet.com/bay/news/
China News Service
   http://www.chinanews.com/cns/
ClariNet e.News
   http://www.clari.net
Croatia News
   http://www.carnet.hr/hr_news/
Czech News Agency
   http://www.ios.com/~jirim/czech.html
Disaster.Net
   http://www.disaster.net/
Egypt News
   http://cybernetics.net/users/asiinc/tem.html
Federal News Service
   http://www.csn.net/~johnhart
Federal News Service (transcripts)
   http://www.fednews.com
Finland (Virtual Embassy)
   http://www.mofile.fi/fennia/um/
Gallup Poll
   http://www.gallup.com
Global Internet News Agency
   http://www.gina.com
Global Student News
   http://www.jou.ufl.edu/forums/gsn/
GrayFire
   http://www.grayfire.com
Great Lakes Environmental Wire
   http://www.cic.net/~glew

Guyana News
  http://cville-srv.wam.umd.edu/~swi/GuyNews/guynews.htm
Hungary Report
  http://www.yak.net/hungary-report/
India News Service
  http://www.genius.net/indolink/INDNews/index.html
Iran Islamic Republic News Agency
  http://www.ncf.carleton.ca/freeport/government/embassies/mid.
  east/iran/News/menu
Jerusalem Data Service
  gopher://jerusaleml.datasrv.co.il
Korea News Service
  gopher://koisnet.kois.go.kr/11/dir6
Kyodo News Service
  http://www.toppan.co.jp/kyodo/
Los Angeles Times–Washington Post
  http://www.newsservice.com
MGN (image library)
  http://www.mgnonline.com
Newsbytes Pacifica
  http://www.islandtel.com/newsbytes/
Newshare
  http://newshare.com:8001/Newshare/welcome.html
NewsUSA (News releases)
  http://www.newsusa.com
New Zealand Press Association
  http://www.rsnz.govt.nz/cgi-bin/news/rsnz/news
Omnivore News Service
  http://ukanaix.cc.ukans.edu/carrie/news_main.html
OneWorld Express
  http://www.oneworld.org/news/news_top.html
Point Now
  http://www.pointcom.com/now/updated.htm
PoliticsUSA
  http://PoliticsUSA.com
Press Association of Britain
  http://www.pa.press.net/
PR Newswire
  http://www.quote.com/info/bwire.html

Reuters NewMedia
http://www.yahoo.com/headlines/current/news/summary.html

Sarajevo Online
http://www.axime.com/wm/sarajevo/onasa.htm

Southlight Photo Agency
http://www.aztec.co.za/slpn/

SportsLine USA
http://www.sportsline.com

Taiwan Central News Agency
http://www.taipei.org/teco/cicc/news/default.htm

Time Daily (Time magazine)
http://www.timeinc.com/daily/time/1995/latest.html

U.S. Information Agency—
gopher://info.itu.ch/11/.1/MISSIONS/.1/US%20Mission/Wireless%20File

Video Online (Italian)
http://www.vol.it

Vogon News Service (British)
http://www.cm.cf.ac.uk/htbin/RobH/Vogon

Voice of America
http://www.social.com/social/index.html

West's Legal News
http://www.westpub.com/lnot

WorldNews On Line
http://worldnews.net/

WWW WorldNews Today
http://www.in.net/sfics/wwwwnt/wnt.html

Your Health Daily
http://nytsyn.com/medic/

BROADCAST NETWORKS

ABC-TV
http://www.abctelevision.com

ABC via Real Audio
http://www.realaudio.com/contentp/abc.html

Association of America's Public TV Stations
http://www.universe.digex.net/~apts/

Bailey Broadcasting Services
http://www.LeeBailey.com

Cable News Network
http://www.cnn.com

CBS Radio
http://www.cbsradio.com

CBS-TV
http://www.cbs.com

CBS Up to the Minute
http://uttm.com

Christian Broadcasting Network
http://www.cbn.com

C-NET Central (USA Network)
http://cnet.com

C/Net Radio
http://www.cnet.com/Central/Radio/

Comedy Central
http://www.comcentral.com/

Corporation for Public Broadcasting
http://www.cpb.org

C-SPAN
gopher://c-span.org/1

Discovery Channel
http://www.discovery.com

ESPN
http://ESPNET.SportsZone.com/

Fox Network
http://www.eden.com/users/my-html/fox.html

Fox Sports
http://www.foxsports.com

fX (A Fox network)
http://www.delphi.com/fx/fxtop.html

Idaho Public Television
http://isuux.isu.edu:80/~iptv/

Internet Multicasting Service
http://town.hall.org/

Learning Channel
gopher://gopher.internet.com:2100/11/category/media/Television/
tlc_monthly/1hilight

Maryland Public Television
http://www.mpt.org/mpt

Monitor Radio
http://town.hall.org/radio/Monitor

National Public Radio
http://www.npr.org

National Public Radio
http://www.realaudio.com/contentp/npr/me.html

NBC-TV
http://www.nbc.com

News Channel
http://www.access.digex.net/~wjla/news8.html

Nickelodeon
http://nick-at-nite.viacom.com

North Carolina News Network
http://www.capitolnet.com/ncnn

Public Broadcasting Service
http://www.pbs.org/

QVC (Shopping)
http://www.qvc.com/

SciFi Channel
http://www.scifi.com

South Carolina ETV
http://www.scetv.state.sc.us/scetv/

Underground Network
http://www.undernet.com

Universal Channel
http://www.mca.com/tv/index.html

UPN
http://www.cs.brandeis.edu/~aaron/upn/upn.html

VH1
http://here.viacom.com/vh1/index.html

Virtual Radio
http://www.microserve.net/vradio/

Voice of America
gopher://gopher.voa.gov/11/newswire

WA1A Global Radio
http://www.wa1a.com

Weather Channel
http://www.weather.com

Wisconsin Public TV and Radio
http://www.vilas.uwex.edu

TELEVISION STATIONS

Albany, N.Y.: WNYT-TV
http://www.wnyt.com/

Anchorage, Alaska: KYES-TV
http://www.alaska.net:80/~fireweed/

Athens, Ohio: WOUB-TV and WOUC-TV
http://www.tcom.ohiou.edu/tv.html

Atlanta: WAGA-TV
http://www.america.net/com/waga/waga_1.html

Atlantic City, N.J.: WMGM-TV
http://www.acy.digex.net/~wmgmtv/

Austin, Texas: KVR-TV
http://www.utexas.edu/depts/output/www/tstv.html

Birmingham, Ala.: WBRC-TV
http://www.traveller.com/wbrc/

Bloomington, Ind.: WTIU-TV
http://www.indiana.edu/~radiotv/WTIU/wtiuover.html

Boise, Idaho: KAID-TV
http://isuux.isu.edu:80/~kisu/kaid.html

Boise, Idaho: KIVI-TV
http://www.kivi-tv.com

Boise, Idaho: KTVB-TV
http://www.primenet.com/~ktvb/

Boston: WABU-TV
http://web.bu.edu/COM/html/wabu.html

Boston: WCVB-TV
http://www.wcvb.com/

Boston: WGBH-TV
http://www.wgbh.org/home.html

Boston: WGBX-TV
http://www.wgbh.org/pages/GBX/GBX.html

Boston: WHDH-TV
http://www.whdh.com/

Bozeman, Mont.: KUSM-TV
http://www.kusm.montana.edu

Buffalo, N.Y.: WKBW-TV
http://www.wkbw.com/

Cedar Rapids, Iowa: KCRG-TV
http://WWW.infi.net/fyiowa/kcrg

Cedar Rapids, Iowa: KGAN-TV
http://www.kgan.com/

Charleston, S.C.: WCIV-TV
http://www.awod.com/gallery/wcivtv4/

Charlotte, N.C.: WCNC-TV
http://www.wcnc.com

Chicago: WGN-TV
http://www.wgntv.com

Chico-Redding, Calif.: KHSL-TV
http://www.pinsight.com/~khsltv/

Cincinnati: WLWT-TV
http://www.wlwt.com

Cleveland: WJW-TV
http://www.zdepth.com/wjw/wjwmain.html

Coeur d'Alene, Idaho: KCDT-TV
http://isuux.isu.edu:80/~kisu/kcdt.html

Colorado Springs, Colo.: KKTV
http://www.kktv.com/

Colorado Springs, Colo.: KXRM-TV
http://www.kxrm21.com/

Columbia, Mo.: KOMU-TV
http://www.missouri.edu/~jschool/komu/

Columbia, S.C.: WOLO-TV
http://www.scsn.net/biz/wolo

Columbus, Ind.: WBC-TV
http://www.cpbx.net/Cable/19news.html

Columbus, Ohio: WBNS-TV
http://www.concourse.com/10tv

Dallas: KDFW-TV
http://www.pic.net/media/kdfw/

Dallas: KTVT-TV
http://www.pic.net/media/ktvt/

Dallas: KXAS-TV
http://www.pic.net/media/kxas/

Dallas: WFAA-TV
http://rampages.onramp.net/~news8/

Denver: KCNC-TV
http://www.kcncnews4.com/

Denver: KRMA-TV
http://www.intel-edge.com/krma/home.html

Denver: KUSA-TV
http://www.aaco.com/9news/

Detroit: WDIV-TV
http://www.rust.net/WDIV/index.html

El Paso, Texas: KVIA-TV
http://www.kvia.com

Eugene, Ore.: KVAL-TV
http://surf.rio.com/~kval/kval.html

Ft. Myers, Fla.: WSFP-TV
http://www.naples.net:80/media/wsfp/

Ft. Wayne, Ind.: WANE-TV
http://www.cris.com/~Wane-tv/

Gainesville, Fla.: WUFT-TV
http://www.freenet.ufl.edu/~wuft/index.html

Grand Rapids, Mich.: WXMI-TV
http://www.iserv.net/wxmi

Green Bay, Wis.: WFRV-TV
http://www.dct.com/WFRV/

Green Bay, Wis.: WGBA-TV
http://www.wgba.com

Hagerstown, Md.: WHAG-TV
http://www.whag.com/

Honolulu: KHON-TV
http://www.khon.com/news/

Houston: KHOU-TV
http://www.khou.com/

Houston: KTRK-TV
http://www.sccsi.com/13/home.html

Houston: KUHT-TV
http://www.kuht.uh.edu/kuht.html

Huntington, W.Va.: WOWK-TV
http://www.ramlink.net/wowk

Huntington, W.Va.: WSAZ-TV
http://www.ianet.net/wsaz

Huntsville, Ala.: WAAY-TV
http://www.hiwaay.net/waay/waay-tv.html

Huntsville, Ala.: WAFF-TV
http://www.traveller.com/waff/

Huntsville, Ala.: WHNT-TV
http://www.nuance.com/whnt/index.html

Indianapolis: WISH-TV
http://www.wish-tv.com/8/

Indianapolis: WRTV-TV
http://www.wrtv.com/wrtv6/

Indianapolis: WTHR-TV
http://wthr.com/13/

Johnson City, Tenn.: WJHL-TV
http://www.tricon.net/Comm/wjhl/index.html

Kingsport, Tenn.: WKPT-TV
http://www.tricon.net/Comm/wkpt/index.html

Lake Charles, La.: KPLC-TV
http://www.maas.net/kplc

Las Vegas: KLAS-TV
http://www.infi.net:80/vegas/KLAS-TV/

Las Vegas: KTNV-TV
http://www.ktnv.com/ktnv

Las Vegas: KVBC-TV
http://www.intermind.net/kvbc/

Lexington, Ky.: WLEX-TV
http://www.mis.net/wlex/wlexmain.html

Little Rock, Ark.: KARK-TV
http://www.cei.net/kark/kark.html

Little Rock, Ark.: KASN-TV
http://www.kasn.com/

Little Rock, Ark.: KLRT-TV
http://www.klrt.com/

Los Angeles: KCAL-TV
http://tvnet.com/TV/CAtv/KCAL.html

Los Angeles: KCBS-TV
http://www.kcbs2.com/

Los Angeles: KNBC-TV
http://www.knbc4la.com/

Madison, Wis.: WISC-TV
http://www.wisctv.com

Memphis, Tenn.: WMC-TV
http://wmcstations.com@vantek.net

Miami: WSVN-TV
http://www.wsvn.com/

Miami: WTVJ-TV
http://www.nbc6.nbc.com

Milwaukee: WITI-TV
http://www.execpc.com/~business/tv6.html

Minneapolis: KMSP-TV
http://tccn.com/kmsp/upn9.html

Minneapolis: WCCO-TV
http://www.wcco.com/

Mobile, Ala.: WALA-TV
http://www.maf.mobile.al.us/media/wala

Mobile, Ala.: WKRG-TV
http://www.wkrg.com/tv5/

Moscow, Idaho: KUID-TV
http://isuux.isu.edu:80/~kisu/kuid.html

Nashville, Tenn.: WSMV-TV
http://www.wsmv.com

Nashville, Tenn.: WTVF-TV
http://www.infi.net/nc5/nc5top.html

Norfolk, Va.: WHRO-TV
http://www.whro-pbs.org/

Norfolk, Va.: WVEC-TV
http://www.wvec-tv13.com/wvec/

Oklahoma City: KFOR-TV
http://www.ionet.net/~kfor/kfor.html

Oklahoma City: KOCO-TV
http://www.ionet.net/koco/index.html

Oklahoma City: KOKH-TV
http://www.kokh.ionet.net

Oklahoma City: KWTV-TV
http://www.kwtv.com/kwtv/

Orlando, Fla.: WFTV-TV
http://www.sundial.net/~wftvch9/

Orlando, Fla.: WOFL-TV
http://www.eyec.com/wofl

Pasco, Wash.: KEPR-TV
http://oneworld.owt.com:80/kepr/

Philadelphia: WHYY-TV
http://libertynet.org/community/whyy/whyy.html

Phoenix: KAET-TV
http://www-kaet.pp.asu.edu/

Phoenix: KNXV-TV
http://www.knxv.com/

Phoenix: KUSK-TV
http://www.kusk.com

Pittsburgh: KDKA-TV
http://www.kdka.com

Pocatello, Idaho: KISU-TV
http://isuux.isu.edu:80/~kisu/kisu.html

Portland, Ore.: KATU-TV
http://www.halcyon.com/komo/fisher.html

Portland, Ore.: KOIN-TV
http://www.koin.com/~koin

Quincy, Ill.: WGEM-TV
http://www.cencom.net/~wgem/

Sacramento, Calif.: KOVR-TV
http://www.kovr.com/

Sacramento, Calif.: KXTV-TV
http://calweb.calweb.com/~kxtv10/

Saginaw, Mich.: WNEM-TV
http://www.cris.com/~wnemtv5

Salisbury, Md.: WBOC-TV
http://www.dmv.com:80/~wboc/

Salt Lake City: KBYU-TV
http://www.byu.edu/tmcbucs/kbyuuniv/gonews.htm

Salt Lake City: KJZZ-TV
http://www.xmission.com/~insearch/kjzz.html

Salt Lake City: KTVX-TV
http://www.xmission.com:80/~ktvx/

San Antonio, Texas: KLRN-TV
http://lot49.tristero.com:80/klrn/

San Antonio, Texas: KMOL-TV
http://kmoltv4.dcci.com/

San Diego: KGTV-TV
http://www.kgtv.com/

San Diego: KPBS-TV
http://wwwnt.thegroup.net/kpbs/kpbstv.htm

San Francisco: KBHK-TV
http://www.upn44.com/

San Francisco: KGO-TV
http://www.kgo-tv.com/welcome

San Francisco: KPIX-TV
http://www.kpix.com/

San Francisco: KQED-TV
http://www.kqed.org/

Schenectady, N.Y.: WRGB-TV
http://albany.globalone.net/wrgb/

Seattle: KING-TV
http://www.halcyon.com/kingtv/welcome.html

Seattle: KOMO-TV
http://www.halcyon.com/komo/chanfour.html

Sioux City, Iowa: KTIV-TV
http://users.aol.com/ktiv4/tube.html

Sioux Falls, S.D.: KDLT-TV
http://www.on-ramp.com/kdlt.html

Springfield, Mass.: WGBY-TV
http://www.wgbh.org/pages/GBY/GBY.html

Springfield, Mo.: KOLR-TV
http://kolr10.com

Tallahassee, Fla.: WFSU-TV and WFSG-TV
http://www.fsu.edu/~wfsu_tv/

Tampa, Fla.: WFTS-TV
http://www.wfts.com/welcome.html

Toledo, Ohio: WBGU-TV
http://www-wbgu.bgsu.edu/wbgu.html

Traverse City, Mich.: WPBM-TV
http://aliens.com/tv7-4/tv7-4.html

Tucson, Ariz.: KUAT-TV
http://info-center.ccit.arizona.edu/~kuat/kuat1.html

Tucson, Ariz.: KVOA-TV
http://www.kvoa.com/

Tulsa, Okla.: WJRH-TV
http://kjrh.com

Tulsa, Okla.: KTFO-TV
http://www.galstar.com/~upn41/index.html

Twin Falls, Idaho: KIPT-TV
http://isuux.isu.edu:80/~kisu/kipt.html

Washington, D.C.: WETA-TV
http://www.weta.org/

Washington, D.C.: WJLA-TV
http://www.access.digex.net/~wjla/wjla.html

Washington, D.C.: WRC-TV
http://www.nbc.com/nbc4dc/

Wichita, Kan.: KAKE-TV
http://www.southwind.net:80/kake/

Wichita, Kan.: KSNW-TV
http://www.southwind.net/ksnw/

Youngstown, Ohio: WFMJ-TV
http://www.zdepth.com/wfmj/

RADIO STATIONS

Albany, N.Y.: WAMC-FM
http://www.npr.org/members/WAMC

Albuquerque, N.M.: KZRR-FM
http://www.94rock.com/kzrr

Anchorage, Alaska: KRUA-FM
http://orion.alaska.edu/www/studorgs/krua/krua.html

Ann Arbor, Mich.: WCBN-FM
http://http2.sils.umich.edu/~pamplona/WCBN.html

Ann Arbor, Mich.: WFUM-FM, WUOM-FM and WVGR-FM
http://www.umich.edu/~wuom

Athens, Ohio: WHLD-FM
http://linus.cs.ohiou.edu/~wlhd

Athens, Ohio: WUOB-AM
http://www.tcom.ohiou.edu/radio.html

Atlanta: WKLS-FM
http://pr.mese.com/radio/96rock/index.html

Atlanta: WNNX-FM
http://PR.Mese.Com/99x

Atlanta: WREK-FM
http://www.gatech.edu/gvu/people/Masters/Lisa.Moore/wrek.html

Atlanta: WZGC-FM
http://www.com/z93/

Baltimore: WBAL-AM
http://www.wbal.com/

Baltimore: WHSR-AM
http://www.jhu.edu/~whsr

Bellingham, Wash.: KUGS-FM
http://pacificrim.net/~kugs/

Berkeley, Calif.: KALX-FM
http://oms1.berkeley.edu/KALX.html

Bloomington, Ind.: WFIU-FM
http://www-iub.indiana.edu/~wfiu/wfiuhome.html

Boise, Idaho: KBSU-FM
http://gozer.idbsu.edu/bsuinfo/news/bsuradio/bsuradio.menu.html

Boston: WBCN-FM
http://www.wbcn.com

Boston: WBUR-FM
http://web.bu.edu/COM/html/wbur.html

Boston: WCRB-FM
http://www.wcrb.com/wcrb/

Boston: WGBH-FM
http://www.wgbh.org/pages/FM/FM.html

Boston: WTBU-FM
http://web.bu.edu/COM/html/wtbu.html

Boston: WXKS-FM
http://www.kissfm.com/kiss/

Boston: WZLX-FM
http://www.wzlx.com/wzlx

Boulder, Colo.: KGNU-FM
http://bcn.boulder.co.us/media/public_broadcasting/kgnu/kgnu-top.html

Bowling Green, Ohio: WBGU-FM
http://www.bgsu.edu/~ckile/WBGUFMhome.html

Bridgeport, Conn.: WPKN-FM
http://www.wpkn.org/wpkn

Buffalo, N.Y.: WBEN-AM
http://www.insv.com/wben/

Buffalo, N.Y.: WBFO-FM
http://wings.buffalo.edu/services/wbfo

Buffalo, N.Y.: WGR-AM
   http://wgr55.moran.com
Burlington, Vt.: WEXP-FM
   http://together.net/~ccb/wexp.htm
Cambridge, Mass.: WMBR-FM
   http://www.mit.edu:8001/activities/wmbr/home.html
Cape Cod, Mass.: WPXC-FM
   http://www.ccsnet.com/wpxc/
Cape Cod, Mass.: WRZE-FM
   http://www.ccsnet.com/wrze/
Champaign, Ill.: WEFT-FM
   http://www.prairienet.org/arts/weft/WEFThome.html
Chapel Hill, N.C.: WUNC-FM
   http://www2.interpath.net/interweb/listenmag/listen.html
Chapel Hill, N.C.: WXYC-FM
   http://sunsite.unc.edu/wxyc/
Charlottesville, Va.: WTJU-FM
   http://www.virginia.edu/~wtju
Charlottesville, Va.: WUVA-FM
   http://minerva.acc.virginia.edu/~wuva
Chicago: WXRT-FM
   http://www.wxrt.com
Cincinnati: WCKY-AM
   http://www.550wcky.com/
Cleveland: WENZ-FM
   http://www.americast.com:80/WENZ/
Cleveland: WMMS-FM
   http://www.wmms.com/wmms
Cleveland: WRUW-FM
   http://litwww.cwru.edu/CWRU/Org/wruw/wruw.html
Clinton, N.Y.: WHCL-FM
   http://www.hamilton.edu/html/news/studentmedia/whcl/whcl.htm
College Park, Md.: WMUC-FM
   http://www.md.edu/StudentLinks/gmoriart/.ljason/wmuc.html
College Station, Texas: KANM-FM
   http://tam2000.tamu.edu/~mdb0213/showdata.html
Columbia, Mo.: KBIA-FM
   http://www.missouri.edu/~jschool/kbia

Columbus, Ohio: WLLD-FM
http://www.concourse.com/wlld/

Corvallis, Ore.: KBVR-FM
http://patriot.wtfd.orst.edu/kbvr-fm/index.html

Davis, Calif.: KDVS-FM
http://www.cs.ucdavis.edu/~swanston/kdvs/current/pg.html

Daytona Beach, Fla.: KISS-FM
http://www.america.com/mall/store/kissfm.html

Durham, N.C.: WXDU-FM
http://nicodemus.mc.duke.edu/wxdu/xduhome.html

East Orange, N.J.: WFMU-FM
http://wfmu.org

Erie, Pa.: WERG-FM
http://theoldman.antioch.edu/default2.html

Eureka, Calif.: KGOE-FM
http://www.northcoast.com/unlimited/services_listing/kgoe/kgoe.html

Evanston, Ill.: WNUR-FM
http://www.acns.nwu.edu/jazz/

Evansville, Ind.: WUEV-FM
http://www.evansville.edu/~wuevweb/wuev.html

Fayetteville, Ark.: KUAF-FM
http://www.npr.org/members/KUAF/

Fayetteville, N.C.: WFSS-FM
http://www.fsufay.edu/WFSS/home.htm

Freedom, Calif.: KPIG-FM
http://www.catalog.com/kpig

Gainesville, Fla.: WRUF-FM
http://www.jou.ufl.edu/about/stations/rock104/

Gainesville, Fla.: WUFT-FM
http://freenet.ufl.edu/ht-free/wuft-fm.html

Geneva, N.Y.: WEOS-FM
http://hws3.hws.edu:9000/weos/

Grand Rapids, Mich.: WGRD-FM
http://www.iserv.net/wgrd/

Grand Rapids, Mich.: WOOD-AM/FM
http://www.woodradio.com

Hamilton, N.Y.: WHCL-FM
http://www.hamilton.edu/html/news/studentmedia/whcl/whcl.htm

Harrisonburg, Va.: WXJM-FM
http://wxjm1.jmu.edu/

Hibbing, Minn.: KADU-FM
http://uslink.net/kadu/home.html

Homer, Alaska: KBBI-AM
http://tundra.alaska.edu/~izkbbi/index.html

Honolulu: KPOI-FM
http://hoohana.aloha.net/edge

Honolulu: KRTR-FM
http://hisurf.aloha.com/QsengStuff/Qseng.html

Houghton, Mich.: WMTU-FM
http://www.hu.mtu.edu/~wdvanloo/wmtu.html

Houston: KRBE-FM
http://www.neosoft.com/KRBE/

Houston: KTRU-FM
http://spacsun.rice.edu/~vek/ktru.html

Houston: KUHF-FM
http://www.kuhf.uh.edu

Huntsville, Ala.: WLRH-FM
http://www.iquest.com/wlrh/wlrh.html

Iowa City, Iowa: KRNA-FM
http://www.netins.net/showcase/krnaweb/

Kalamazoo, Mich.: WKFR-FM
http://www.wkfr.com

Kalamazoo, Mich.: WKMI-AM
http://wkmi.com

Kalamazoo, Mich.: WRKR-FM
http://www.wrkr.com

Kankakee, Ill.: WONU-FM
http://www.olivet.edu/Campus/Departments/WONU/WONU.html

Kent, Ohio: WKSU-FM
http://www.wksu.kent.edu/

Knoxville, Tenn.: WUOT-FM
http://denali.cti-pet.com/WUOT_docs/WUOT-homepage.html

Knoxville, Tenn.: WUTK-FM
http://solar.rtd.utk.edu/stream/services/sradio/nrock.html

Lansing, Mich.: WKAR
http://wkar.msu.edu

La Mirada, Calif.: KBBK-FM
http://www.biola.edu/orgs/kbbk/index.html

Las Vegas: KUNV-FM
http://www.unlv.edu/KUNV/

Las Vegas: KVBC-FM
http://www.kvbc.com/kvbc

Lawrence, Kan.: KJHK-FM
http://www.cc.ukans.edu/~kjhknet/index.html

Lexington, Ky.: WUKY-FM
http://www.uky.edu/WUKY/wuky.html

Long Beach, Calif.: KLON-FM
http://www.csulb.edu/~klon/

Los Altos Hills, Calif.: KFJC-FM
http://www.cygnus.com/misc/kfjc.html

Louisville, Ky.: WFPL-FM
http://www.npr.org/members/WFPL/wfpl.html

Lynn, Mass.: WLYN-AM
http://www.shore.net/~wlyn/welcome.html

Medford, Mass.: WMFO-FM
http://www.tufts.edu/~wmfo/

Melbourne, Fla.: WA1A-FM
http://www.wa1a.com/

Melbourne, Fla.: WTAI-FM
http://www.wtai.com/public/wtai.html

Memphis, Tenn.: WMC-AM/FM
http://wmcstations.com@vantek.net

Miami: WKIS-FM
http://wkis.com

Miami: WQAM-AM
http://wqam.com/

Middletown, Conn.: WESU-FM
http://www.con.wesleyan.edu/groups/wesu/wesu.html

Milwaukee: WKTI-FM
http://www.execpc.com/wkti/

Milwaukee: WYMS-FM
http://www.mixcom.com/folkdj/index.html

Minneapolis: KEGE-FM
http://nic.mr.net:3085/edge/

Minneapolis: KFAI-FM
http://www.mtn.org:80/KFAI/

Murfreesboro, Tenn.: WMOT-FM
http://www.mtsu.edu/~wmot/

Myrtle Beach, S.C.: WKZQ-FM
http://city-info.com/wkzq.html

Nashville, Tenn.: WKDF-FM
http://cutting.edge.net/

Newark, Del.: WVUD-FM
http://www.udel.edu/nero/wvud.html

New Orleans: WWOZ-FM
http://www.webcom.com/~gumbo/wwoz-sched.html

New York: WCBS-AM
http://www.newsradio88.com

Oberlin, Ohio: WOBC-FM
http://www.physics.oberlin.edu/sunbird/wobc.html

Omaha, Neb.: KVNO-FM
http://www.kvno.unomaha.edu

Orlando, Fla.: WUCF-FM
http://www.npr.org/members/WUCF/

Paradise, Nev.: KNUU-AM
http://www.vegas.com/knews/hompag.html

Peoria, Ill.: WCBU-FM
gopher://bradley.bradley.edu:70/11/Media%20Services/WCBU-FM

Philadelphia: WFLN-FM
http://beethoven.com/wfln

Philadelphia: WHYY-FM
http://libertynet.org/community/whyy/whyy.html

Philadelphia: WXPN-FM
http://www-penninfo.upenn.edu:1962/penninfo-
srv.upenn.edu/9000/1295.html

Phoenix: KDKB-FM
http://www.netwest.com/kdkb

Phoenix: KEDJ-FM
http://www.getnet.com/kedj/

Phoenix: KHTS-FM
http://www.giaco.com/khits

Phoenix: KIDR-AM
http://www.giaco.com/kidr

Phoenix: KUPD-FM
http://www.netwest.com/kupd

Phoenix: KVRY-FM
http://www.kvry.com

Phoenix: KZON-FM
http://www.kzon.com/

Pittsburgh: WRCT-FM
http:///afs/andrew.cmu.edu/usr/wrct/www/home.html

Pittsfield, Mass.: WBEC-FM
http://www.am1420wbec.com

Plover, Wis.: WIZD-FM
http://members.aol.com/wizdfm/index.html

Portland, Ore.: KBOO-FM
http://www.teleport.com/~kboofm/

Portland, Ore.: KPSU-AM
http://www.ee.pdx.edu/other/kpsu/

Provo, Utah: KXRK-FM
http://www.x96.com/

Quincy, Ill.: WQUB-FM
http://www.quincy.edu/WQUB/welcome_wqub.html

Raleigh, N.C.: WRAL-FM
http://www2.interpath.net:80/wralfm/

Red River, La.: KDAQ-FM
http://www.npr.org/members/KDAQ/

Richmond, Va.: WCVE-FM
http://freenet.vcu.edu/arts/wcve-fm/wcve-fm.html

Rochester, N.Y.: WXXI-AM
http://www.npr.org/members/WXXI/wxxi.html

Rohnert Park, Calif.: KSUN-FM
http://www.sonoma.edu/ksun/

Rolla, Mo.: KMNR-FM
http://www.umr.edu/~kmnr

Rolla, Mo.: KUMR-FM
http://mercury.cc.umr.edu:80/~kumr/

Sacramento, Calif.: KFBK-AM
http://www.kfbk.com

Salt Lake City: KBZN-FM
http://www.kbzn.com/breeze/

San Diego: KMKX-FM
http://www.electriciti.com/~danlopez/

San Diego: KPBS-FM
http://www.thegroup.net/kpbs.htm

San Diego: KSDT-FM
http://waynesworld.ucsd.edu/KSDT/KSDT.html
San Francisco: KDFC-FM
http://www.tbo.com/
San Francisco: KITS-FM
http://www.hooked.net/alex/radioa.html
San Francisco: KJAZ-FM
http://www.dnai.com/~lmcohen/kjaz.html
San Francisco: KPIX-FM
http://www.kpix.com/
San Francisco: KQED-FM
http://www.kqed.org/
San Francisco: KUSF-FM
http://www.usfca.edu/usf/kusf/kusfhomepage.html
San Jose, Calif.: KSJS-FM
http://www.rahul.net/ecat/ksjs.html
Santa Cruz, Calif.: KSCO-AM
http://human.com/radionet/
Santa Cruz, Calif.: KSCU-FM
http://www.iuma.com/kscu/index.html
Seattle: KIRO-FM
http://www.halcyon.com/kiro/hello.html
Seattle: KJR-FM
http://www.halcyon.com/normg/kjr_fm.htm
Seattle: KMPS-FM
http://fine.com/kmps
Seattle: KOMO-AM
http://useattle.uspan.com/komo/entertainment-news.html
Seattle: KUOW-FM
http://www.kuow.washington.edu/kuow.html
Socorro, N.M.: KTEK-FM
http://nmt.edu/~ktek/
South Bend, Ind.: WVFI-AM
http://www.nd.edu/StudentLinks/jlyons/WVFIstuff.html
Stanford Village, Calif.: KZSU-FM
http://kzsu.stanford.edu/
Swarthmore, Pa.: WSRN-FM
http://sccs.swarthmore.edu/~justin/Docs/WSRN.html

Telluride, Colo.: KOTO-FM
http://infozone.telluride.co.us/InfoZone/Town/koto/koto.html

Thousand Oaks, Calif.: KCLU-FM
http://robles.callutheran.edu/KCLU.html

Tucson, Ariz.: KEKO-FM
http://biz.rtd.com/keko/

Tulsa, Okla.: KWGS-FM
http://www.utulsa.edu/KWGS/

Wake Forest, N.C.: WAKE-FM
http://www.wfu.edu/Student-organizations/WAKE-
Radio/index.html

Waltham, Mass.: WBRS-FM
http://www.wbrs.org/

Washington, D.C.: WAMU-FM
http://soundprint.brandywine.american.edu/~wamu/

Washington, D.C.: WETA-FM
http://soundprint.brandywine.american.edu/~weta/

West Lafayette, Ind.: WBAA-AM/FM
http://www.cis.purdue.edu/cisfiles/cis-home.htm#wbaa

Wichita, Kan.: KFDI-FM
http://www.elysian.net/kfdi/kfdi.htm

Wichita, Kan.: KICT-FM
http://www.elysian.net/t95/t95.htm

Wilmington, Del.: WSTW-FM
http://www.ravenet.com/wstw/

Winston-Salem, N.C.: WFDD-FM
http://www.wfu.edu/Administrative%20offices/WFDD%20Public%
20Radio

Worcester, Mass.: WPIR-FM
http://www.wpi.edu/~radio/

Youngstown, Ohio: WYSU-FM
telnet.wysu.html

Ypsilanti, Mich.: WEMU-FM
http://www.emich.edu/public/wemu/index.html

INDEX